Children in
WAR

Children in
WAR

by **ALAN** and **SUSAN RAYMOND**

TV Books
New York

Library of Congress Cataloging-in-Publication Data

Raymond, Alan.
Children in war / by Alan & Susan Raymond.
p. cm.
Contents: Bosnia—Israel—Rwanda—Northern Ireland.
ISBN: 1-57500-098-9
1. Military history, Modern—20th century. 2. Children—History—20th century.
3. Atrocities—History—20th century. I Raymond, Susan. II. Title.
D842.2.R39 2000
303.6'6'08309045—dc21
99-089374

TV Books, L.L.C.
1619 Broadway, Ninth Floor
New York, NY 10019
www.tvbooks.com

Interior design by Tania Garcia
Manufactured in the United States of America

OVERLEAF: *War ravaged city of Mostar, Bosnia,
with temporary rope bridge across the Neretva River.*

FOLLOWING PAGE: *Bosnian boy and girl in city of Mostar.*

Dedicated
to all the children in war
around the world
for a future in peace

contents

introduction

The twentieth century has been the most violent in world history. One measure of the severity of modern warfare is the toll it has taken on children. According to a recent report issued by the United Nations entitled "The Impact of Armed Conflict on Children," two million children have been killed in wars around the world in the last ten years. In the same period, another four to five million were disabled, twelve million were left homeless, and one million were orphaned or separated from their parents. The report went on to say that an estimated ten million children in war were psychologically traumatized and that today 50 percent of the world's refugee population are children.

"These statistics are shocking enough," said Graca Machel, the author of the report, "but more chilling is the conclusion to be drawn from them: more and more of the world is being sucked into a desolate moral vacuum. This is a space devoid of the most basic human values; a space in which children are slaughtered, raped and maimed; a space in which children are exploited as soldiers; a space in which children are starved and exposed to extreme brutality. Such unregulated terror and violence speak of deliberate victimization. There are few further depths to which humanity can sink."

As documentary filmmakers, this report inspired us to make a television program that would inform and move audiences to think about the plight of these boys and girls in war zones. We wanted people in the United States to see how children in faraway countries experience war and terrorism and not be indifferent to their plight. We wanted to make a documentary that would provoke thoughtful discussion and change, and persuade everyone—from ordinary citizens to government leaders—to focus more attention on the problem.

At the beginning of the twentieth century, civilians accounted for only 15 percent of all war casualties. In World War II, 50 percent of those who died were civilians. Today, 90 percent of those killed or wounded in war are civilians, mainly women and children. Wars are no longer waged by armies on a battlefield; wars are not fought between nations, but within them.

These so-called "unwinnable wars" are ethnic civil wars and territorial conflicts that are fought in streets, villages, and cities and that can quickly degenerate into the slaughter of helpless civilians.

There have been more than 150 wars fought since World War II, and there are approximately thirty wars going on right now in different parts of the world. We traveled to four of them—Bosnia, Israel, Rwanda, and Northern Ireland—to interview children caught in military and terrorist conflicts. We believe their experiences are similar to those of millions of other children around the world also living in countries embroiled in armed conflict, terrorism, or war. These could be the voices of the children of Kosovo, East Timor, Pakistan, Bangladesh, Chad, the Sudan, Syria, Chechnya, Ethiopia, the Philippines, Nigeria, Burma, Sierra Leone, Congo, Burundi, or Sri Lanka. The list goes on.

In the documentary, we ask children to describe their war experiences in an effort to tell us all something about the state of the world at the end of the twentieth century. We want them to speak for themselves, to describe their lives and what it is like growing up in a war zone. By hearing the stories directly from these boys and girls, the film shows first-hand accounts from the children about their suffering. The documentary also deals with peace and conflict, psychological trauma, revenge and retribution, injustice and abuse, and humankind's follies. As filmmakers, we do not intend to suggest simple solutions to such a complex problem, nor can we resolve the dilemmas that underlie the horrific situations from which the film is drawn.

If it is true that wars show humankind at its very worst and its very best, then we believe the children's interviews in the documentary show them at their best. Even though many of the boys and girls we interviewed suffered terribly and endured tremendous hardships, they maintained a generous human spirit, an admirable resilience. None of them was filled with hate or sought revenge against those who had harmed them. Many of the children did ask for justice in the face of evil and for an end to the hatred that started these wars. These child survivors have inherited the task of rebuilding their countries' futures. Perhaps years from now, when these children are adults and are offered an opportunity to become the next generation's leaders, they will do so with compassion and tolerance.

This book is an adaptation of the documentary film we produced and directed for HBO which is also entitled "Children in War." The book contains many more children's interviews than we could include in the film. It also contains interviews with child psychologists and social workers who specialize in helping children suffering from war-related trauma. The interviews are accompanied by children's drawings, writings, and poems describing their experiences in Bosnia, Israel, Rwanda, and Northern Ireland.

The principles of protection for children in wartime have been established by international humanitarian law. The Fourth Geneva Convention and the Convention on the Rights of the Child both define standards for ensuring the care and safety of children in armed conflicts, but guarantees of human rights for children are often violated by governments and ruthless military leaders. Children were deliberately targeted and killed in the four conflicts depicted in the documentary. The United Nations has finally begun to establish a legal and moral framework that will create new categories of war crimes affecting children. These crimes against humanity would be prosecuted by an international court of law. The world can no longer remain indifferent to the plight of these boys and girls. Clearly a renewed commitment is needed on behalf of children in situations of armed conflict. Peace is every child's right.

These very special children in war can tell us some underlying truths about our current moral universe. As more time passes, the more valuable their interviews will be. It is our hope that the interviews in this book will stand for future generations as significant collective memories that capture the madness of wars fought at the end of the twentieth century.

— Alan and Susan Raymond
January 2000

bosnia

The violent disintegration of Yugoslavia became the most vicious conflict in Europe since World War II. Militant ethnic nationalism led to a brutal war fought between the republics of Serbia, Croatia, and Bosnia. Lasting from 1992 to 1995, the war in Bosnia was characterized by extreme violations of international humanitarian law. The siege warfare of ethnic cleansing inflicted upon its civilian population was both shocking and horrifying. An estimated fifteen thousand children were killed, many of them deliberately targeted.

During the war in Bosnia, children were systematically shot at by snipers, terrorized by relentless bombing and shelling, and forced to flee burning villages; many witnessed their parents or friends being killed, and often, in the case of young girls, were sexually abused. There were no "safe havens" for the children in Bosnia. Many suffered grave injuries, both physical and psychological. Boys and girls lost their childhood, saw too much, and endured too much anguish and pain. At the same time, many of Bosnia's children displayed amazing resilience in the more than three years of war. Against all odds, they showed both strength and dignity when confronted with mortal danger.

Less than a hundred miles from Sarajevo, Mostar is a five-hundred-year-old city that sits in a narrow, mountainous valley. Bosnia's third largest city, it is divided in half by the Neretva River, and its most famous landmark is the Stari Most or Old Bridge. Completed in 1566 in what was then part of the Ottoman Empire, the bridge was for hundreds of years a symbol of the unity between cultures in the former Yugoslavia. Bosnian Muslims, Croats, and, to a lesser degree, Serbs lived together in Mostar. There were also marriages between people of different ethnic groups. But the harmony and peace of this multi-ethnic city dramatically unraveled with the onset of the war.

Mostar first came under attack by the Serbian army after Bosnia declared independence from Yugoslavia. Serbian people fled the city as it became no

OPPOSITE: *The famous Stari Most Bridge in Mostar, completed in 1566, withstood earthquakes, floods, and two world wars, only to be destroyed by Croatian artillery in the 1990s.*

longer safe to live there. The Muslim and Croatian militias joined together and successfully defended their city against the Serb forces. Then Croatia declared war on Bosnia, and Mostar became a violently divided city as Croats and Muslims turned their guns on one another. As the children of Mostar looked on in alarm, neighbors they had known or lived with for years became their feared enemies. Families were forcibly evicted from their homes overnight. The Croats took control of the west side of the city and drove the Muslims into a ghetto on the east side of the Neretva River.

During the Croat-Muslim siege, Mostar endured eleven months of relentless bombardment that reduced the city center to ruins. The Stari Most Bridge, which had withstood earthquakes, floods, and two world wars, was destroyed by Croatian artillery. The destruction of the ancient bridge symbolically ended the centuries-old link between the two cultures in the former Yugoslavia and became a sad monument to the demise of tolerance in the Balkans.

It was against this dramatic backdrop that we commenced filming during the last year of the war in Bosnia. We arrived in Mostar during one of many ceasefires when all fighting was suspended for a week or two as mediation continued. These ceasefires inevitably ended, usually without any forewarning. People were busy stockpiling food provided by relief agencies, children were actually playing outside for the first time in months, and even young couples were getting married and driving through the streets. Everyone knew that this freedom would end, and the uncertainty of the future never really left the public consciousness. But at least for a time, people could move about the city in relative safety.

What we saw made a deep impression upon us. Every park, playground, and open space in Mostar had been turned into a makeshift graveyard. Many of the simple wooden grave markers were those of dead children. Gazing on grave markers dating from 1989 to 1994 was hard evidence of the war's toll. On block after block of the city, nothing remained but the skeletons of buildings standing among enormous mounds of rubble. Every inch of every wall of these destroyed buildings was splattered by shells and grenades.

In the Muslim ghetto of East Mostar, the buildings which people were living in were extensively damaged. Few had intact windows or doors. Gaping holes in the walls or roofs were covered with plastic sheets. There was no electricity or running water in this half of the city. A makeshift system of open spigots on the street had been set up for people to collect water. Children were the ones usually sent to do this. It was a very risky errand for they exposed themselves to shelling and snipers, and many children were wounded or killed while performing this simple task.

For most of the war, children lost their chance to play. They were forced to live for long periods of time in temporary underground bomb shelters or cellars, or they were kept inside by their parents for safety's sake. But with the ceasefire in place, there were kids everywhere on the streets: jumping rope, kicking soccer balls, climbing on the bombed-out mounds of rubble, or just running around. It was as if they were making up for three years of lost playtime.

In the midst of all this rubble was a little boy with a huge grin on his face, chasing a soccer ball. His name was Sanel. He was a twelve-year-old, blond, blue-eyed Muslim boy with a very outgoing personality.

He told us a little of his family's history. They were displaced, driven out of their home village of Gacko by the Serbian army or, as he referred to them, "the Chetniks." The family fled to Macedonia but were again driven out by the Serbs. Eventually they came to West

Mostar to live with a cousin but was once more forced to leave, this time by the Croatian militia or, as Sanel called them, "the Ustashas." Sanel and his family finally ended up in East Mostar where they took a fully furnished, abandoned apartment that another family had fled. This was a common practice as approximately half of the city's population was living in apartments or houses that weren't originally their own.

Sanel was very good at concealing his war injury by tucking his sleeve into his trouser pocket. It wasn't until we were talking with him for a few minutes that we realized he was missing an arm.

Interviewer: What would you say to children who don't know what it's like to live in war?

Sanel: I would like to tell children wherever they may be, God forbid that they have to live what we've gone through in Bosnia. God forbid that shells would fall near them all the time.

It's very difficult to live in war. You just wait for the moment you will die.

One night we were waiting for Dad to come home from work. Mom was sitting between us and we had fallen asleep. Shells were constantly falling around the house. You didn't even hear the shells fall.

My pajamas and pillow and bed were all bloody. My arm was hanging by a piece of skin and I came to the terrace and fell down. My mother took me in her arms and brought me to the medical center where they had to perform surgery immediately. But there was no electricity at that moment.

That is when my life was in limbo—would I live or would I die? And just at that time, the generator went on. My arm was full of shrapnel and they operated.

They couldn't save my arm—the shrapnel had ripped apart all the bones and nerves. I stayed in the hospital for a long time—a month.

I felt very good. But when I awoke after they had given me an injection that put me to sleep to operate on me, I felt that my arm was in a cast. My mother told me that they cut off my arm and that I shouldn't be upset. My mother sat next to me that entire night.

Interviewer: Is your arm OK now? [*Sanel's arm was amputated just above his elbow.*]

OPPOSITE: *Sanel, age 12, who lost an arm to a shell in Mostar, Bosnia.*

Sanel: Da [*Yes*].

Interviewer: Did you cry when you found out about your arm?

Sanel: I didn't cry because it could have been worse. If you consider what could have happened, I'm lucky to be alive. I have some use of my arm. I can work with it and get around.

I don't know. I'm not to blame for it. But what can you do? A shell doesn't have any eyes. What can I say? It happened.

Sanel was somewhat atypical in his acceptance of his war injury. The loss of an arm or a leg can create anxiety and fear in the mind of a child, largely in anticipation of another attack or explosion. Severe war injuries in children can also cause feelings of embarrassment or shame, with the injured child not wanting to leave the house or meet people. Although there is most often an eventual acceptance and adaptation to the changes in a wounded child's body, it can be very traumatic for the child for a long time. Everyone can see a physical war injury, whereas psychological trauma can be repressed or covered up. Several other children we interviewed in Mostar who suffered the loss of a limb were much less accepting of their injuries and, in fact, displayed quite a bit of anger and bitterness toward the people who caused the injury.

During the intense shelling of the city, all hospitals, schools, mosques, and churches were deliberately targeted and the children of Mostar missed a year and a half of school. All of the schools were heavily damaged, and the school in

East Mostar was completely demolished. In the third year of the war, however, the children's education was slowly returning to normal thanks largely to the emergency assistance of an organization called Swiss Disaster Relief. It was rebuilding schools in both East and West Mostar, and some children were once again attending classes on a fairly regular basis.

The schools provided the children of Mostar with a sense of returning normality and structure in their daily lives. More importantly, schools are useful settings for the practice of art therapy, one of several techniques that can help children cope with their fears and anxiety. In war zones such as Mostar, all of the children witnessed terrifying incidents of cruelty and death.

Because a child is still developing psychologically, witnessing traumatic events can damage them even more severely than physical wounds. Repeated traumatization, as often happens in war, can also deform the self-identity of a child, causing him or her to lose hope and optimism, forever influencing how he or she views the world. The earlier the trauma occurs in a child's life the more crippling to the personality structure. The resulting psychological damage, known as post-traumatic stress disorder, can last a lifetime and is difficult to heal. Unlike grief, time alone will not erase the trauma.

However, war-related trauma is not irreversible and not all children suffer from it equally. Every child has different strengths and weaknesses, causing him or her

to cope well in some circumstances but poorly in others. It's a complicated emotional state of mind and one that is not fully understood by child psychologists. Much more research is needed to understand how some children seem resilient despite trauma, while others seem so vulnerable and incapacitated.

What is clear is that to help them cope, children in distress should be given an opportunity to express themselves through drawings, writing, role-playing, and discussion. Helping children express their emotions is crucial to alleviating severe trauma. The very act of drawing or talking about their war experiences will begin a healing process.

All the Bosnian drawings reproduced here are from one class of ten-year-old children in a West Mostar elementary school. Their teacher had encouraged them to make a series of pictures recalling events they had witnessed during the war. Some drew battle scenes, others showed houses burning and people fleeing. A few sketched detailed drawings of specific incidents they remembered, such as the death of a friend.

The following children tell such stories.

Marin: My name is Marin Smajac. I'm ten years old. I drew this picture to depict the death of my best friend Nino. He and I were playing ball and my older brother told us to leave. But we didn't want to leave and then a shell fell. Nino was killed. And my other friend Sasha was wounded and the rest of us all lived, thank God.

That was the worst day for me. I didn't have anyone to play with.

Then my mother, brother, and sister went to Split [*a city on the Dalmatian coast of Yugoslavia not affected by the war*]. We stayed in Split for a month. When we returned, refugees were living in our home. Then we slept in the basement while the shells were falling. We couldn't leave the basement because we might have been killed. My father didn't let us play so we just sat in one place.

Interviewer: Were you afraid?

Marin: Yes, I was afraid that a shell might fall through the windows. There were no sandbags covering the windows. I was scared. My father had just left for the battlefield. I waited to see if he would return alive and healthy. My father left with the army. He never came back.

Interviewer: Do you know where your father is now?

Marin: I don't know.

Interviewer: Do you think that you are a very brave person?

Marin: Yes.

Interviewer: What would you like to do in your future?

Marin: I would like to be an actor.

Interviewer: Who is your favorite actor?

Marin: Arnold Schwarzenegger.

Ines: My name is Ines Kostic. I live in the city, in Mostar. I am ten years old. I'd like to read this message to you:

> The war arrived. My city is destroyed. The old beauty no longer exists. People die. The enemy destroys everything. They aren't asking themselves whether their own children will ever forgive them when they discover that their fathers destroyed the happiness of the innocent. Those are heartless people. You can't even call them human beings, they're beasts. An old saying befits them: "Animals are sometimes better than humans." I hope this damn war ends and that the enemy pays for all that they did.

I drew my apartment building when the enemy was destroying it. In the hearts on the picture is written that the rain of peace is falling and sends a message to the enemy to end the war and not to destroy the innocent, the happiness of the innocent.

Marin, age 10.

Ines, age 10.

This is my apartment building as it is burning down. Here is the blood of my best friend when she was killed by a sniper. I was very sad when she died. That was the worst day of my life. I was barely able to go to her funeral because I was so upset. I even threw up at one point, I felt sick watching her burial. It was very difficult for me.

It's difficult for me to talk about that. That was the worst day of my life.

She was my best friend. We always played together. Now it's difficult without her. Her name is Jelena. We played with Barbie together. We studied together. Before the shell killed her, we used to go to the bomb shelters together. We had a good time playing together, we went to school together, we did everything together until she was killed.

Interviewer: Were you close by when it happened?

Ines: Well, yes, I was nearby. I heard it from the window. Shells were falling very close by. I wanted to see from what direction they were shelling us. I saw a small house from where a sniper was shooting and I saw how my friend wanted to enter her apartment building . . . she was running across the street . . . but the sniper shot her.

It was very difficult for me. I couldn't accept my friend's death for many, many days. It was very difficult.

What do I think of the enemy? How can they destroy others' happiness?

They have their own city, their own children but can destroy others. Why don't they think of their own children? How can they not feel sorry about killing other people's children? I think they are truly beasts. They are not human beings.

I am always angry and mad and unhappy. I am always unhappy whenever a friend of mine dies. When the enemy shells my city, I'm incensed. I can never forgive them because that which they did to us can truly never be forgiven.

Andrea: My name is Andrea. I am ten years old. I'm from Mostar. I drew this picture because it somehow reminds me of Mostar more than anything else. [*Andrea's drawing shows the Stari Most Bridge blown apart.*]

While I watched them destroy the old bridge, Mostar is all I could think of. I will never, never forget that image. When our teacher told us to draw something related to the war, I immediately thought of this. I thought of everything relating to Mostar. The burning of the bridge disturbed me the most.

When I was small, I always went over to the other bank with my mother. I passed over the bridge many times. I was very unhappy when it was destroyed. It was once very nice for me here in Mostar.

I had a wonderful childhood. I went to school here. I had many friends and it was wonderful. I truly felt good in my hometown. I never felt that way elsewhere. Of all the cities I've visited, something always brings me back here.

Now.... Well, now it's destroyed. It's nothing like it had been before. The buildings have been destroyed, the houses burned. People somehow act differently—they're nothing like they were before the war. They have a certain expression on their faces, as if they are unhappy. I guess that's because their loved ones were killed during the war. The war changed everything.

Interviewer: Why do you think they shelled the bridge?

Andrea: I don't know. Probably because the bridge is an important symbol of Mostar; it is tied to the city. The name of the city of Mostar is said to have derived from that bridge.

Interviewer: Do you think it can be rebuilt?

Andrea: I think it can. Everything can be rebuilt, as long as the war ends and peace ensues. Everything can be rebuilt with some love and willpower—everything can be rebuilt. I think my friends had a hard time accepting that everything is different now. But I think everything will be OK if the war ends and peace comes to us. I think we could all be happy again.

Interviewer: What is most important to you now?

Andrea: The establishment of peace, the stopping of war is the most important thing. That everyone—that all the children—return to their homes and that everything is peaceful. That there is an abundance of love and good will to rebuild and that everything becomes beautiful as it had been before.

Interviewer: Does something frighten or disturb you or your friends when you think about the war?

Andrea: Yes. I often wake up abruptly and remember the horrors my friends and I lived through. Many of my friends are now living in foreign countries. I don't think they will ever forget those horrors; the memories will always be with them.

While in West Mostar, we met two brothers, Goran and Zoran, twelve and fourteen years old. Like many others, they had been forced from their village by an invading army, except in this case, Goran and Zoran were Croats and the invaders were a Bosnian Muslim paramilitary unit. These two boys witnessed the death of their family and were captured while hiding in the forest. The child-

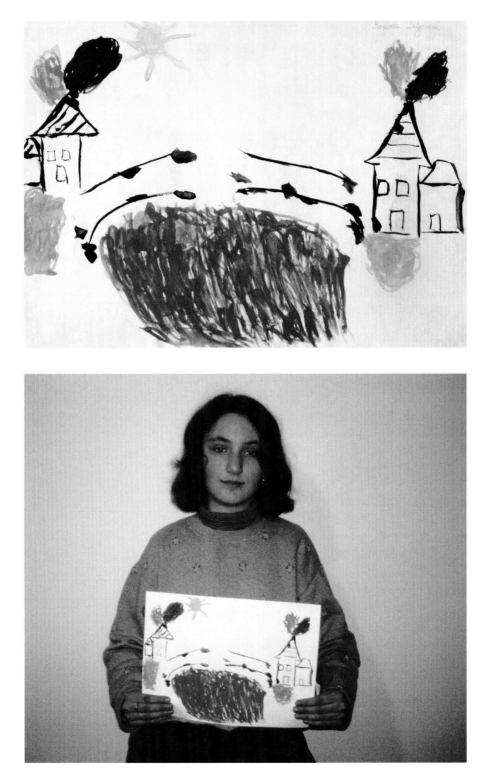

Andrea, age 10.

MOSTAR
PSYCHO-SOCIAL SURVEY OF CHILDREN

(Published by UNICEF Office of the Special
Representative to the Republics of the former Yugoslavia)

Results of War Trauma Screening:

85% of children have been forced to leave their town or village during the war.

57% reported that one or both of their parents were wounded.

19% have been injured.

19% have siblings that have been injured.

62% have seen dead bodies.

90% have seen someone who was injured in the war.

95% have been in a situation during the war in which they thought they would be killed.

100% have experienced shelling very nearby.

75% have had their homes attacked or shelled.

67% had been shot at by snipers.

43% have experienced serious food and water shortage.

24% reported they thought they would die from the cold.

Trauma Reactions:
Results show that frequently:

53% of children think life is not worth living.

71% have terrifying dreams.

77% have experienced stomachaches; this may be evidence of extreme hunger or may be psychosomatic.

Goran, age 12, and Zoran, age 14.

ish action of running away had saved their lives. The brothers were eventually reunited with their uncle in Mostar.

Goran: Those mountains in Grabovica...it was always nice in the mountains. The air was fresh...it was always nice. And then, when the war started, we used to play less. There was shooting in the forest. You couldn't leave the house.

Zoran: Even before the enemy came into Grabovica, things weren't so good. First our [*Croat*] soldiers attacked them in Dreznica. The next day [*the Bosnian army*] attacked Grabovica and stole whatever could be taken. They mistreated us. They even beat some people. You didn't have the most basic elements with which to live—whatever you wanted to eat, they would steal. And when the new soldiers [*the paramilitary unit*] came later, they asked us if we were Croats and we said we were. And then they killed everyone. We ran into the forest.

Goran: I was scared. When they came to fight, I said we should hide. And I was telling my mother to hide. Maybe things wouldn't end so well, I told her.

Nermin Divovic, a seven-year-old Bosnian child, was killed by a sniper.

She said, "Yes. I know. Everything has changed here. Soldiers often come to drink coffee in our house, so these will probably leave after a while also." I never believed this. I would always hide when the soldiers came.

The soldiers asked our family if we had any livestock. We said we did. They told mom and dad to show them the livestock. I heard a round of bullets being fired. I told my brother we should hide in the forest. Things wouldn't end well. We hid. We heard voices and gunshots. I tried to go back to the house two or three times but I couldn't do it. I was scared. Bullets were falling close to me.

The soldiers were probably from Sarajevo; they were Muslims. We walked around the forest for half the day. We went to our neighbor's house. We were hungry by then. We came down from the forest, but didn't quite reach the house.

At one point, I had an opportunity to run down toward the neighbor's house. When I saw that everyone had been killed in there—it belonged to our neighbor Josip—I got so sick to my stomach that I ran back into the forest and told my brother that our neighbors probably weren't alive. That no one is left alive. We waited there in the forest a bit and then we returned to our house. We came close to our house and looked around. We saw soldiers walking around the house, keeping watch. We went back up into the forest and waited again.

We stayed in the mountains for a long time. It was already getting dark. The soldiers stumbled across our hiding place and they saw us running away. They whistled and told us to sit down, that they wouldn't hurt us. I asked a soldier if we could go home and get some clothing. We got near our house but the soldiers told us not to go in there. He said there were dead bodies there and we shouldn't look at them. But we did go into our house and took what we could.

As we were leaving, I saw that my mother and sister had been killed. We saw my father, grandmother, and grandfather were murdered. The soldiers took us away from the house. We came to a place where there were many soldiers. They asked us if we were hungry. We said that we were. We ate and spent the night there. They questioned us in the morning. There were about one hundred, maybe more, soldiers there. They threw us in a car and drove us to the outskirts of Jablanica. Then we waited to see where they would tell us to go. We told them that we had an uncle in Jablanica and that we wanted to go to him. They said OK, fine, and then we waited.

They took us to Jablanica and we stayed there for four or five months. A prisoner exchange between the governments of Croatia and Bosnia took place and we were finally relocated. And then we came here to Mostar with our uncle.

Interviewer: How will you remember your mother and father? What is your fondest memory of them?

Goran: It's hard for me to remember. Sometimes I think that everyone is here and gathered together. Then I realize that no one is here, that everyone has been killed. I can't imagine that this has happened. What the soldiers did makes no sense.

Zoran: How would I remember them? I can't possibly describe it. When I think of them I feel both happiness and sadness equally.

In the more than three years of war in the former Yugoslavia, an estimated 200,000 people were killed and 3,000,000 people became refugees or displaced persons. The extremist nationalist ideology of ruthless military leaders practicing "ethnic cleansing"—a deliberate effort to end the existence of a specific group of people—terrorized the civilian population of the former Yugoslavia. Ordinary men, women, and children were brutally expelled from their villages and their land seized. This forced movement exposed the refugees to the dangers of shelling, snipers, torture, rape, illness, and starvation.

The refugees were exiled throughout the former Yugoslavia and Europe.

Bosnian Muslim refugees being expelled from their village by Serbian army forces.

After the Dayton Peace Accord which ended the war, fewer than 10 percent of these refugees would ever return to their homes. These forced population displacements were not simply the consequences of the war in Bosnia, they were the war's main purpose. The refugees' lives were disrupted, probably beyond repair. They are now supported entirely by international aid and have, in the most optimistic view of the situation, an unknown future.

For children, this can be a devastating life change. Their normal lives effectively ended. They left behind their homes, usually with little or no notice. Toys and cherished possessions—links to their childhood—all had to be abandoned overnight. In the best of circumstances, they left with their families intact. In many cases, however, fathers or older brothers were separated from the women and children. The fate of the men remains unknown, although it is a reasonable assumption that they were taken away to be killed. How difficult it must be for refugee children to accept the truth that they can never go home again, that things will never be the same.

Elvisa, age 13.

The town of Varazdin, once the ancient capital of Croatia, is home to one of the many refugee camps in the country. About fifty miles north of Zagreb, Varazdin is a medieval town with extraordinary churches and castles. The refugee camp, however, is a totally depressing, dark structure that was once a Yugoslav army barracks. Surrounded by twisted, dead trees and a bleak cement-covered courtyard, Varazdin camp has become a temporary residence primarily for Bosnian Muslims expelled by the Serbian army. It is terribly over-crowded; families live in very close quarters with nothing more than blankets on clotheslines to separate their beds from one another. Each family is allotted cots and a few square feet of space. Some have lived there for as long as three years. Each family tries to personalize their space with pictures, small toys, and the few cherished belongings they managed to carry when fleeing their homes. The best one could say is that they are safe and no longer in the battlefield.

Of the many children we interviewed at Varazdin, three are included in this book. They are all teenage girls, each with a different story to tell. The first is Elvisa, a thirteen-year-old who was taken to the infamous "death camp" Trnopolje. At Trnopolje, which literally means "field of thorns," men, women, and children were imprisoned in the most dire of circumstances. Given little or no food and water, housed in huge rooms with no privacy, sleeping on the floor, the detainees at Trnopolje were subjected to torture, beatings, and other atroc-ities at the hands of the Serbian guards. Women and young girls were repeat-edly raped and sexually abused as a deliberate tactic of oppression.

Interviewer: Tell us about the day you had to leave your home.

Elvisa: We were in the house. We knew there was going to be a war. They came to our village. We had all gathered in my house. And when they came into the village, they were yelling, telling us to get out of the house. We came out.

And they wanted to take all of us to the mosque. They wanted to burn us alive. But they had already burned the mosque. We went to a house and stayed there. I thought they were going to kill us. We were lucky.

Interviewer: What army came?

Elvisa: The Serbs were already there. We had to leave. They were shoot-ing, burning, destroying things there.

They separated the men and took them away. I don't know where. Then they came and told us we had to leave the village. We left. We were in a city and they shoved us on buses. They didn't tell us where we were going.

Then they brought us to a camp called Trnopolje and we stayed there. The men were taken to Omarska where there is also a camp. They killed the men there.

Interviewer: What happened to your father?

Elvisa: They took him away and we know nothing of his whereabouts.

Interviewer: What do you think happened?

Elvisa: [*Shrugs.*] I don't know.

Interviewer: Could you tell us more about that camp? How did the soldiers treat you?

Elvisa: Well, they had encircled us. They were around the camp Trnopolje. We went outside and played. When young women came outside, soldiers would look them over. They looked like they wanted to take them away.

At night the Serbs came into our room. They would take a young woman and rape her and mistreat her. When we wanted to fetch water, they wouldn't let us pass through. All they kept saying was how they were going to kill us.

Interviewer: Did you think they were going to kill you?

Elvisa: Yes.

Interviewer: Is it difficult to talk about these memories?

Elvisa: Yes.

Almedina, age 14, with her younger brother.

Almedina is fourteen years old and came to Varazdin from Sarajevo. Like Elvisa, she is a Bosnian Muslim. Almedina and her mother, teenage brother, and baby brother escaped from Sarajevo through a tunnel that the Bosnian people dug under the Sarajevo airport. People would crawl through this tunnel and climb over Mount Igman, a mountain controlled by Bosnian forces but under Serbian army fire. Snipers would shoot at people as they entered or exited the tunnel. This was a very dangerous trip and one that many people did not complete. Almedina, her mother, and baby brother then fled to central Bosnia and later to Croatia, where they finally reached Varazdin.

Almedina: My name is Almedina. I am fourteen years old. I have been here at the center for three months. I lived in Sarajevo for three years and I left Sarajevo in November 1994. My mother and two brothers and I left Sarajevo because life was too hard there. And it was very difficult with the baby. My father stayed. He is a soldier in Sarajevo.

We didn't take a direct bus from Sarajevo to Zagreb. First we used the tunnel underneath the airport's airstrip, of which I'm sure you've heard. We walked through the tunnel for maybe half an hour and then we climbed Mount Igman and a bus was waiting for us there and it brought us to Zagreb and then we came here to Varazdin.

That was the only way for us to get out. It's a very short tunnel—you can't walk upright. We had to bend over as we walked. It's very stuffy inside. We barely got through that tunnel, and we also had some things that we had to carry with us. It was very difficult while we were passing through, underground. It's also very narrow so two people couldn't pass one another.

My little brother could walk by then, so that it was easiest for him to get through the tunnel. Because he was little and short, he could walk normally. Snipers shoot at the entrance and exit to the tunnel; they can't shoot while you are underground. They were shooting the night we left but, thank God, none of us were hurt.

We had to wait until the shooting stopped and then we climbed the mountain but they shoot at the mountain as well. We couldn't take the risk and climb the mountain right away because there was shooting. No one wanted something to happen to him or her. It doesn't sound that terrible when you speak about it now, but I am amazed that we lived through all that. Everything is so peaceful here, by contrast.

In Sarajevo we lived in an apartment. There were two bedrooms, a living room, and a kitchen. During the war, we all had to stay in one room—we only used one room and the bathroom. A sniper was shooting into the other rooms so we couldn't even enter those rooms. Because there was non-stop shooting then, we had to leave our apartment and move to the neighboring building, where there was an apartment that was not as damaged as ours and we could use two rooms there.

Then for heat. . . . We didn't have anything with which to heat ourselves. At the beginning of the war, they would sometimes give us a little heat. But then we stripped metal from stores, metal shelves for example. We took that metal and made a wood-burning stove. We burned everything we had in the apartment—dressers, all the furniture, dolls, toys, books. Basically, we burned everything we owned. We even burned our clothes, just to stay warm. Eventually, we ran out of things to burn. All the trees in the park had been cut down. There are many people in Sarajevo and no one has anything with which to heat their homes. There isn't a wooden bench left in the city. Whatever was wooden, whatever could burn, can no longer be found.

I saw quite a lot of people being wounded or killed. In the entrance to the building in which I lived, two or three people were wounded, and we all watched that.

We watched people get wounded from our windows. That's how it was. Those are very disturbing sights. People were wounded and begged for help but no one could get close to them to help them. No one could help them because bullets or shells were falling on all sides. Regardless of how much we wanted to help—and everyone wanted to help one another—we just couldn't because the vast majority of those streets are exposed to sniper fire. You are never sure when you'll be the next target and you are constantly afraid. You can't leave the house.

One of the worst things I witnessed was the shelling of a soccer game. It was Bajram, and I was getting ready to visit a friend, because it's a custom for us to visit one another's homes on holidays. But my father told me to wait; that we would go together. They were telling us not to go outside over the radio, because it was feared that because it was a Muslim holiday, there would be a lot of shooting. But people didn't believe this. Regardless of how much shooting took place, what kind of people could possibly lob yet another shell? So everyone gathered at a soccer game and then a shell fell.

All of a sudden, the screams and cries started. Everyone had someone dear to them at that soccer game and someone was always losing a loved one. Women were running out barefoot to see what had happened to their children, because people were coming from the soccer field all bloody—both those carrying the wounded and those not carrying anyone. It was terrible. Everybody was crying that day. It was difficult for everyone.

I would like to move back. I would like to see people live as they had lived before because—regardless of the material damage—all of that could be repaired and I think life could once again be what it had been. Only if the Serb forces would pull back their guns, to let people live their lives. I have many, many fond memories. There were nice moments we shared together even at the height of the war. I have memories as would anyone else about the city in which he or she lived, in which he or she was born. There will always be happy memories.

Selma is only twelve years old. She is also a Bosnian Muslim. Her family was expelled from the Bosnian town of Modric. They fled in UN trucks that were evacuating people from the intense fighting in that area of Bosnia. During her trip, the UN trucks came under heavy attack from Serbian fighter planes that were dropping bombs on the convoy. Selma's perceptions of war are haunting and poignant.

Selma, age 12.

Interviewer: Can you describe what your life was like before the war?

Selma: How was my life? Well, it was normal. Life was like it always is when you're at home. It was good. Until the war started.

Interviewer: How long have you lived in a refugee camp?

Selma: In Varazdin? Two years and maybe four months.

Interviewer: Is your family all together?

Selma: No. My mother, brother and I are here, but my father was killed.

Interviewer: Can you tell us how that happened?

Selma: In Orasje.

Interviewer: Was your father a soldier?

Selma: Yes.

Interviewer: What do you think of the soldiers who killed your father?

Selma: Those soldiers surely liked to kill. If the soldier who killed my father also has a child, I hope his child does not have to suffer the way I have had to. He was a good man. He always wished the best for people. He loved us.

War. War. Whoever hasn't experienced it doesn't know what it is. When they destroy your home or kill a loved one, or when there's shooting. When there is no food or water, when you don't have your freedom. The war is taking place because someone doesn't want us to be in our homes. Because some people wish for evil.

israel

Although some of the children in Israel would describe the situation there as a war, it is more accurate to say that Israel is a country in which terrorism has been part of the fabric of life for both Palestinian and Israeli children since the state's founding. On a daily basis there is a palpable sense of terror for the Israeli people. At the same time there is the daily sense of oppression for the Palestinian people. Israel is the homeland of two peoples. Both Arabs and Israelis feel the land belongs to them, and their ongoing struggle to co-exist in the country has created one of the most bitter and protracted international conflicts in modern history. In recent years, there has been a slow but steady progress toward a resolution to the conflict, one that would provide for some kind of a Palestinian state alongside Israel, with mutual guarantees of peace and security. In our documentary, we tried to present both sides of the story.

The Jabalia refugee camp in Gaza has been in existence since 1948 when Palestinians fled their homelands during the war that led to Israel's statehood. Palestinians refer to this historical event as the Nakba, or "catastrophe." Intended as a temporary facility in 1948, more than fifty years later three generations of children have grown up in the Jabalia camp.

It is one of the poorest and most densely populated areas in the world. More than 100,000 Palestinians live here, and over half of them are children under the age of fourteen. The Jabalia camp is an environmentally degraded area in which to live. It has poor sanitation and marginal health care; disease and infection are rampant. The housing is shoddy and makeshift. Jobs are scarce; 40 percent of the people living there are unemployed. There are eight similar refugee camps in Gaza.

The Gaza Strip was occupied by Egypt until the Six Day War of 1967, when it fell to the Israelis. Although some parts of Gaza, including the Jabalia camp, were eventually returned to the Palestinian Authority under the terms of the Oslo Peace Accord in 1993, many Palestinian people lived under military oc-

OPPOSITE: *The Jabalia refugee camp in Gaza.*

Bilal, left, and Mohammed, right, both took part in the Intifada.

cupation for their entire lives. As a consequence, this protracted life under military occupation led to the politicizing of Palestinian children. It was in the Jabalia camp, in December 1987, that the Intifada started.

Palestinian children rebelled against the Israeli army which had occupied Gaza for over twenty years. The Intifada or "uprising" began spontaneously when Arab children confronted fully-armed Israeli soldiers by throwing stones at them. This primitive but effective protest focused world attention on the struggle of the Palestinian people. Lasting seven years, the Intifada would eventually lead to the withdrawal of the Israeli army from Gaza.

But the "children of stones" paid a terrible price for their part in the Intifada. They were also its main victims. Shot at with both live ammunition and rubber bullets, teargassed and beaten, one out of every five boys in Gaza between the ages of eleven and fifteen was seriously injured at the hands of the Israeli army. Many of the children who participated were traumatized by the events they witnessed. Although the Palestinian children in Jabalia no longer live under military occupation, the emotional wounds and deep psychological impact of that time still linger. For many Arab boys, the memory of the years of Israeli army occupation still causes an intense animosity.

We interviewed two teenage boys named Bilal and Mohammed on the streets of the Jabalia camp in Gaza. Both boys took an active part in the Intifada.

> **Bilal**: Of course, most of my childhood from seven to thirteen I have
> spent during the Intifada. Everyone participated. All the children

ABOVE, TOP AND FOLLOWING PAGE: *A Palestinian child's drawings
of the occupation of Gaza and the Intifada.*

ABOVE, BOTTOM: *An Israeli soldier restrains a Palestinian child during the Intifada.*

Palestinian boys in Hebron.

were part of it. My generation's role was merely to throw stones and confront the occupation.

Mohammed: By God, it's a difficult life here. Very difficult here. During the Jews' time, there were the stones, the tanks, the tear gas. And then they killed us.

Interviewer: Why did you throw the stones? Why did you do that?

Bilal: All of the suffering we had was because of the occupation. No one could stand by and watch those terrible happenings. The Israeli army despised the whole population. It didn't matter whether you were young or old. The army used to go into our houses without permission, beat the owners, the neighbors. Show no mercy to anyone in the house. They would break the furniture, destroy even the kitchens, and then harm the young and the old.

Mohammed: We threw stones. They shot us. They broke into our house. They took my brothers and my father to the police station. Two days before the army left, they caught me and beat me badly.

Interviewer: Weren't you afraid you were going to be hurt or arrested?

Bilal: When one used to see how the soldiers hurt people and abused them, that took away all the fear. Especially for the children. They had a lot of guts. And they wanted to sacrifice themselves to raise people's morale and to get back at those enemies who mistreated the whole Palestinian people.

Mohammed: When you're ten years old and saw what the Jews did and how they shot at us, we couldn't be numb. Seeing people we knew were bleeding. We were shot at many times, but that only made us attack more. Yes, I was shot twice. We couldn't stand still seeing our brothers and neighbors bleeding. I saw one who was shot and killed. We have to liberate Palestine and its people.

Interviewer: Do you think you will ever live peacefully with the Israelis?

Bilal: Inshallah. [*If God wills it.*]

While in Gaza, we interviewed Dr. Mustafa, a psychologist at the Gaza Community Mental Health offices. He specializes in treating Palestinian children affected by traumatic experiences such as they had during the Intifada.

Dr. Mustafa: The children in Gaza during the Israeli occupation had restricted freedom of movement, education, and normal child development. School closures were too long, two and a half years long. The children were not free to play. The only activity was to confront the army by throwing stones at them. Anxiety and insecurity prevailed. Many saw family members beaten. Ninety-five percent of the children had at least one traumatic incident.

There were night raids on homes. Four percent had bones broken, especially limbs, intentionally inflicted by the Israeli army. Seeing their fathers beaten or humiliated was more serious than physical wounds. It is more traumatic to a child to lose his role model. The father's loss of dignity caused psychological trauma such as depression, anxiety, and post-traumatic stress disorder.

Symptoms were mostly those of fear—fears of all kinds, not only related to soldiers and the Intifada. They had sleep terrors and nightmares, bed-wetting. Parents described aggressive behavior and violent tendencies in 30 percent of the cases. They became withdrawn and isolated and tended to play alone or were shy and fearful. They had both emotional and behavioral problems.

It was not a structured home or school situation but rather chaotic. Teachers and parents were no longer effective role models to their kids. The children became interested only in politics and Intifada-related activities. In their early teens, children begin to formulate their own identities and social models. The most important role models during the Intifada were martyrs or fugitives wanted by the authorities.

Children took things into their own hands. It was a struggle in which adults were not so prominent. It is not usual or normal. It's not healthy. Development is not normal in the area of struggle or politics. The effect is that those children became politicized. They all know who's who in politics but in real education and development, they are deficient. The situation itself was abnormal. The adults were also frustrated and had lost respect in the eyes of the child.

The child regresses to his grandiose fantasies. He will do it himself. He is the one to do it. Nobody else is doing it so he will do it. They went in the streets and started making war with the soldiers. It no longer was a fantasy but a reality. It was actualized in the streets by seven- and eight-year-old children throwing stones.

These children emotionally need to live a normal life and be raised in a healthy environment with socially approved behavior. They are having problems catching up in school and are not used to dealing with a teacher as a teacher. Of these children, 12 percent have some psychological problem and 30 percent have symptoms of psychological problems or behavior problems. These children still have wounds that have not healed. Such experiences need venting and need to be put into perspective.

Actually, for those who participated in the early years of the Intifada, they had very high self-esteem. But after a few years of the Intifada, studies showed exactly the opposite. Active participants had lower self-esteem and more psychological problems.

For those children who participated in the first stages of the Intifada, it was something of a healing process of frustration that vented the children's anger. Later those active children had more trauma in that they re-traumatized themselves every time they confronted the army.

Twenty miles south of Jerusalem is the West Bank city of Hebron, an ongoing flash point of Arab-Israeli violence. It is one of the oldest cities in the world, dating from 2000 B.C.E.

In Hebron, a few hundred heavily-guarded Jewish settlers live among 120,000 Palestinians. Hebron is the only city in the West Bank where Israelis and Palestinians live together. The militant Israeli settler movement considers Hebron its spiritual capital. This belief is based upon an ancient temple the Jewish settlers call the Tomb of the Patriarchs. It is a holy place for both Jews and Muslims. Arabs call it the Abraham Mosque. It is believed to be the burial place of the biblical figures Abraham, Isaac, and Jacob. The shrine is the focal point of the city and is a bitterly contested place of worship for the Arabs and Jews who live in Hebron.

Sitting on a hillside above Hebron is a large and controversial Jewish settlement of five thousand people called Qiryat Arba. Liberal Israelis feel Qiryat

---

**GAZA COMMUNITY MENTAL HEALTH PROGRAMME SURVEY
OF CHILDREN WHO PARTICIPATED IN THE INTIFADA**

92.5% were exposed to tear gas.

42% were beaten.

55% witnessed beatings.

4.5% had bones broken.

85% were exposed to night raids.

19% were detained for short periods of time.

**IMPACT OF THE OSLO PEACE
TREATY ON PSYCHOLOGICAL WELL-BEING**

After the signing of the Oslo Peace Treaty, the majority of the children in Gaza hope that the peace will bring them true freedom. However, most are unable to envision a friendship with Israeli children. Psychologically, the level of Palestinian children's neuroticism was significantly lower after the peace treaty was signed and their self-esteem was raised. Another finding was that the more actively the children participated in the Intifada, the more their self-esteem increased due to the treaty.

Arba and settlements like it are obstacles to peace. For militant Jewish nationalists, Hebron is the front line in their struggle for the land of Israel. In stark contrast to the ancient city of Hebron, Qiryat Arba is a collection of modern high-rise apartment blocks with wide streets and gardens which would not be out of place in any suburban community.

The children of Qiryat Arba are growing up in a well-protected setting, sheltered from the daily reality of Arab-Israeli tensions. Their schools are modern, well-equipped structures. Nadav, an eleven-year-old boy, attends one of the settlement's elementary schools.

Interviewer: What is it like for you when you leave the settlement and go to the town?

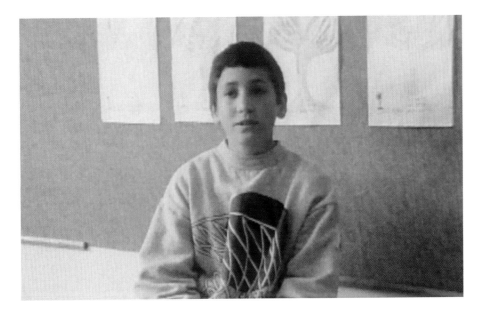

Nadav, age 11.

Nadav: Recently, like about a month ago, we were on the road. Before they cleared Hebron, the Arabs would make these gestures at us of a finger crossing the throat, like this [*Nadav demonstrates the throat-slitting gesture*]. That was very disturbing for us. And they would throw a lot of stones. But more scary than anything were the gestures they made. They would do this. [*Nadav demonstrates the throat-slitting gesture again.*] Meaning that they'll kill us.

Interviewer: And what do you think about those people who did that?

Nadav: What do I think of that? It's scary. Because you're thinking that it's scarier than when they throw stones. Because you feel like at any moment someone can come and harm you whenever he feels like it. When they're doing these gestures at us and they don't even care, it's very scary.

Interviewer: Do you think that you will stay?

Nadav: Yes, I'm certain I'll stay. Our faith keeps us strong. We have a mission that the land of Israel will be ours. We have the faith to stay here.

The Jewish settler movement re-established its current presence in Hebron after the Six Day War. In 1972 they built the Qiryat Arba settlement outside the city. In 1979 a small group of militant Jewish settlers were able to move back to Hebron into the Beit Hadassah, an old hospital facility in the then-ruined Jewish quarter of the city. This was the first time since the 1929 Palestinian massacre of sixty-seven Jews in Hebron that Jewish people were able to live in the ancient city.

The Palestinian Authority took control of 80 percent of Hebron in 1997 under the Israel-PLO (Palestinian Liberation Organization) accord to expand Arab self-rule. The Israeli army, which had occupied all of Hebron for thirty years, now controls the remaining 20 percent of the city. The area they patrol includes the city's Arab vegetable market, the main thoroughfare to the Tomb of the Patriarchs, and the small enclave of militant settlers living in the Beit Hadassah.

The children of the Beit Hadassah settlement walk the streets of Hebron under watchful Israeli army guard. Since 1967 more than thirty settlers have been attacked and killed by Palestinians in Hebron. Nevertheless, the settlers are determined to maintain their presence within a hostile Arab population.

Fourteen-year-old girls Rivka, Nichal, Amia, and Liba are all members of this militant settler group in Hebron.

Interviewer: What happens when you walk through the streets?

Rivka: What's supposed to happen? Sometimes there are exceptional instances when stuff happens, but in general it's normal. We walk through.

Nichal: We walk around free.

Interviewer: Has anyone in your community ever been attacked?

Amia: Yes, my dad. He walked out of a store and someone stabbed him. It was a store he went to all the time.

Rivka: Here, almost everyone was hurt one way or the other. But there are those that were hurt more severely. Three Arabs attacked one settler with axes. He was really in critical condition. But then there are those who are only hurt by stones.

Interviewer: Are you afraid?

All Four Girls: Of course.

Liba: And the day it happens everyone is all shook up. And then things go back to normal. It happens a lot, unfortunately.

Rivka: The day it happens, we feel anger towards the Arabs. Fear.

Nichal: Anger towards the government too. And sometimes we also think we shouldn't go out anymore. But there is no choice. We must. Every time they throw stones, we want to retaliate. If we don't do anything, they'll just keep throwing those stones forever.

Interviewer: You live in a very hostile situation and the current political

CLOCKWISE FROM TOP LEFT: *Amia, Rivka, Nichal, and Liba, all age 14.*

climate makes your future a little uncertain. And I wonder, do you think it's worth the risk?

All Four Girls: Yes. Yes.

Nichal: Of course it's worth it. We care about what happens with the country. It's more of a concern for us. Also, it's part of our struggle actually to live here.

Liba: A kid in Tel Aviv, for example, he won't spend his afternoon taking a PLO flag off a pole. And we sometimes have to do that. Or to fight back, let's say, when they throw stones at us. So we throw stones back at them. A kid in Tel Aviv, it's not what concerns him.

With us, we have a goal. It's not just that we come here to piss off the Arabs or the government. We have a goal to live here. And we are trying to stick to that goal as much as we can. There are also those lefties [*liberal Israelis*] who don't really hate us. They're concerned about us. So they tell us to leave. But if we leave here, it won't be because of fear or anything like that.

Nichal: We're not going to leave.

Liba: No. First of all, we're not going to leave. If and when we do . . .

Nichal: Not even if. Simply we won't.

Liba: If they force us off, then . . .

Nichal: It'll have to be with force. We will never willingly leave here.

Directly across the street from the Beit Hadassah settlement is the Quortaba Elementary School. Two hundred and fifty Palestinian girls between the ages of six and fourteen attend the school. The school, like all buildings in Hebron, is an older structure and is covered with Star of David graffiti painted by the settlers. The Beit Hadassah settlers are determined to close down Quortaba and prevent its students from displaying their Palestinian flag. The settlers often harass the girls on the street coming to school and when going home from school. Settlers also try to seize the Palestinian flag whenever it is displayed. Because of this, many of the younger girls are afraid to go to school.

We interviewed several Palestinian girls in a classroom at the Quortaba School. They are all thirteen years old.

First Student: Usually when we leave school, the army is in the Dabouyah. [*The Dabouyah is the street in front of the settlement.*] But when the settlers tried to harass us, there was not one soldier in the Dabouyah. The settlers were all over the place. They attacked us. A group of them, young and old, hit us with sticks and stones. And they pulled our hair and pushed us down on the ground. Some of them even took out their knives to scare us, that they would kill us with them.

Interviewer: Do you hope that someday you and the settlers will live together peacefully?

Second Student: No, of course there is no hope or way that we would live together. We can't live with them. That is one of the biggest impossibles. They are our enemies. They expect that Hebron and the Abraham Mosque are theirs. But the mosque is ours and it's impossible to allow them to take it.

Interviewer: What do you think the future holds for you in Hebron?

Third Student: We don't have a future because the settlers destroyed our future. They try to make us leave this country and keep it to themselves. But this country is for us and for them as well. I hope there

A class at the Quortaba Elementary School.

will be peace and that we can get rid of all those problems because it only means more trouble for all of us.

Fourth Student: The situation we are living in is the biggest war. On our way to school, the settlers and their kids are always in our way. What Goldstein did in the Abraham Mosque massacre is the biggest proof that we are living in a war situation.

This Palestinian student is referring to an incident in 1994 when Baruch Goldstein, a settler from Qiryat Arba, burst into the Abraham Mosque in Hebron and shot twenty-nine Muslims dead while they were at prayer. Over one hundred children were present in the mosque during the massacre. Seven Arab children under ten years of age were murdered by Goldstein. Moaz, a twelve-year-old boy, was praying with his father in the mosque on the day of the killings.

Moaz: My father's name is Abdel Ibrahim Aljabari. He was killed at al-Haram al-Ibrahimi [*the Abraham Mosque*]. We were kneeling in prayer when the Jewish settler came into the mosque. The first grenade he threw exploded next to the Imam. The second grenade exploded in the middle of the people praying.

And then the settler, who was dressed as a soldier, started shooting. People started screaming "Allahu Akbar." People were falling on the ground. I ran and hid behind the coffins of Ibrahim and Izhaq.

My father saw me going away. He tried to call me, "Moaz, Moaz." A bullet hit him in his chest. When the shooting finished, I got up to

Moaz, age 12, holding a portrait of his father, Abdel.

see my father. He was moving his hands and his legs like this [*Moaz waves his arms*]. I said, "Speak to me." He couldn't talk to me.

Interviewer: Can you ever forgive Goldstein for killing your father?

Moaz: No, no. I don't forgive him. I don't forgive him. My father is gone and my memories of him are fading. What can I tell you? I don't forgive him. It was very painful for me.

   I always think about the massacre. Sitting at my desk at school, that is what is on my mind. I was the first in my class but I am not anymore. I can't study. I am sad about my father. I keep thinking about him.

Moaz in class at the Alshariyeh Boys School in Hebron.

Interviewer: [*To his mother.*] What do you do to settle him down?

Mother: He gets up at night and holds the bars of the window. I get up and wake him from his dream and ask him why he is holding the bars. And he says, "I am dreaming that I am holding a Jewish guy and I want to kill him, the guy who killed my father."

I calm him down. I tell him his dad is a martyr and now he is with God. That my son should take care of his health and his studies. What can I tell him? May God have mercy on his father.

The militant Islamic Resistance Movement, better known as Hamas, enjoys widespread support in Hebron. The group's military arm is one of the most feared terrorist groups in the world because of its campaign of suicide bombings in Israel in recent years. But Hamas is also a charitable organization that runs schools, health clinics, and child care centers for poor Palestinians. Moaz attends the Alshariyeh Boys School run by Hamas in Hebron.

On the day we filmed Moaz's interview, his teacher was arrested for questioning by the Israeli authorities. There had been two recent suicide bombings in Jerusalem and the response to this was a renewed enforcement of strict safety measures. We interviewed some of Moaz's fellow classmates.

Interviewer: What do you think about the current situation here in Hebron?

First Student: We got used to things. We got used to the killing and ar-

Students at the Alshariyeh Boys School.

resting of our fathers. The army enters our houses by force and arrests many, especially those from Hamas. We support those attacks. Yes, we support Hamas. We support Hamas and all its actions.

Interviewer: Are you saying that you support the recent bombings?

First Student: Yes, we support Hamas. We support Hamas and all its actions. They are not doing anything wrong. The Jews do much more to us like the mosque massacre and killing of Yahya Abu Ayash. [*The boy is referring to a well-known Hamas terrorist who was assassinated by the Israelis. They placed a bomb in Ayash's cellular phone and blew his head off.*]

Second Student: They are right about the attacks because if an Israeli kid or two were killed, tens of Palestinian kids have died.

Interviewer: Were you surprised that two of the suicide bombers came from Hebron?

Third Student: No. Here in Hebron it's normal. Nobody was surprised.

Fourth Student: The bombings didn't achieve anything for us. On the contrary, the last suicide bombing operations, if they continue, may hurt us. But if the attacks continue and continue, then finally they may bring results to evicting the Jews from our land. And it will become our land.

Fifth Student: Life in Hebron is very difficult, and we wish that the set-tlers would leave us so that we can get our life back again. Maybe things would get even more difficult for us if Hamas stopped fighting.

Sixth Student: What are our families guilty of to put them in prison be-cause of the attacks? Our fathers, brothers, and teachers, what are they guilty of? They didn't arrest the family of the man who did the Abraham massacre. They didn't demolish their house. But for us, whoever does an attack, they arrest all his family and de-molish his house.

Seventh Student: It's the peace process that has led to these problems. Hamas opposes the peace process. Hamas fights against the peace process. The current situation that the peace process created is very bad. We support Hamas. The peace process didn't achieve anything for us.

Moaz lives in a house with a small terrace that overlooks the Qiryat Arba settlement. As Moaz struggled with the loss of his father, he often looked out from his terrace at Qiryat Arba across the street. Within the enclosed com-munity, the settlers had erected an elaborate shrine to Baruch Goldstein at his gravesite with an epitaph calling him a martyr with "clean hands and a pure heart."

More than five years after it was erected, on December 29, 1999, the Israeli government demolished the shrine, in keeping with legislation known as the Goldstein Law, banning monuments that honor perpetrators of terrorism.

On February 25, 1996, the first day of our filming in Israel, a nineteen-year-old Hamas terrorist from Hebron strapped fifteen kilograms of TNT to his body and boarded a crowded bus in Jerusalem. He detonated the suicide bomb and killed twenty-six passengers. It was the deadliest attack by a suicide bomber in Israel's history. The strike apparently was in retaliation for the Israeli assas-sination of a master Hamas bomb maker known as "the engineer." During the three weeks of filming in Israel, three suicide bombs exploded, one a week. It was highly unusual for the bombings to be that frequent. The Israeli govern-ment believes these attacks are deliberate threats to the peace negotiations. Since the signing of the Oslo Peace Accord in 1993, 253 Israelis have been killed in terrorist attacks.

Nineteen other people riding the bus were critically injured. At the Hadassah Hospital in Jerusalem after the bombing, we met twelve-year-old Yasmin, who was waiting for word about her brother Sarid whose lungs were torn apart by

ABOVE AND OPPOSITE: *Scenes from a
bus bombing in Jerusalem on February 25, 1996.*

the bomb. Yasmin's mother was at her side. They came from Qiryat Shemona, a town in upper Galilee very close to the Israel-Lebanon border. Qiryat Shemona is often targeted by the Iranian-backed Shi'a terrorist group Hezbollah, or Party of God. We spoke first with Yasmin's mother.

Interviewer: How do you help her calm her fears when she gets upset?

Mother: Well, I'm letting her talk about it. And at night when she's afraid, she can hold me; she can be with me; she can talk about it; she can cry. That's OK. That's all.

Interviewer: And how are you doing?

Mother: So so, you know. Sometimes I'm so strong; sometimes I'm crying because I never understood really what parents say to their kids in bed after such a terrible wounding. I still don't believe that he's there. He's so strong. He's so full of life. His beliefs are so hard. You see all his friends praying for him all day. I believe he will survive. He's so strong. His beliefs are strong. He believes in God and in the Torah, and we hope for him.

Interviewer: And what do you think about the person who did this?

Mother: I'm not angry. It's a war. I know it's a war. I hope it's going to be peace in Israel and at last we'll be in peace, real peace. It's a terrible cost. I know that they fill their minds in hate. And I know they're growing up hating, they are suiciders. How can you be angry? They are not normal people. They are doing things that . . . all

Yasmin, age 12.

the years that they grow up...they say...we have to kill the Jews. You know it's not a normal situation.

Yasmin: I always said it would never happen to us. Always. Suddenly it came in such a big boom.

Interviewer: What do you think about the person who did this?

Yasmin: I hate him. I am angry at him. But he's dead. So it's too late to say anything to him. He's dead and a lot of others are dead too.

Interviewer: Do you think you live in a warlike situation?

Yasmin: Yes. Because of the Katyusha rockets. You can always hear the booms when they raid the terrorist camps. The Hezbollah camps. It's like a war, exactly like a war.

Interviewer: Do you ever think of living someplace else?

Yasmin: I love Qiryat Shemona but I also hate it there because of the Katyusha rockets and the war there. There is a lot of tension. Sometimes there are infiltration attempts. Sometimes there are Katyusha rockets. It's scary. Very scary.

Interviewer: What kind of help can you get so you're not so afraid?

Yasmin: When my mommy is by my side I am never afraid. And at school they talk to us about what's going on in the world. They explain things to us. So it helps, too.

Interviewer: What would you tell children who've never experienced this kind of terrible incident?

Yasmin: That they're better off never experiencing it. It's hard. It's painful. It's dead people. It's wounded people. And with God's help, may it end.

In Yasmin's hometown of Qiryat Shemona, we interviewed some of the children at the local elementary school. One of them, a six-year-old boy, showed us the bomb shelter underneath the school, a secure space where the school children hide whenever there is a threat of a Hezbollah rocket attack. These surprise attacks have resulted in the deaths of civilian men, women, and children. Hezbollah is one of the most dangerous terrorist groups in the world and has been responsible for horrific deeds, such as the bombing of the U.S. Marine barracks in Beirut in 1983. In recent years they have tended to confine their efforts to a campaign of terror in the southern part of Lebanon, near the border between Israel and Lebanon.

Professor Mooli Lahad, an Israeli psychologist specializing in the study of Israeli children's war-related trauma, is the director of the Community Stress Prevention Center in Qiryat Shemona. He offered his insights on the effects of this wartime climate on the children of the area.

Interviewer: What effects does the conflict have on children living in this border area?

Prof. Lahad: For children who live in this area there are two kinds of reactions. The short-term reaction is dramatic and frightening. Following an attack, changes occur in children such as fear, stuttering, or immediate stress reactions. But most of these symptoms will disappear in six weeks or so—until the next attack.

The long-term effect is one of prolonged trauma—recurring nightmares, lack of concentration, staying near parents. They feel there is more threat to life. It is like a game of chance—next time it might be you to get it. They feel an extra burden of alertness. Where will I hide? More than half of these children feel it has an effect on their lives. It eventually will reduce their resilience.

Coping studies have shown that children use an emotional approach by talking it over or writing a poem. Some use fantasy or daydream to put the event out of their minds by using their imaginations. Others attach themselves to media information to relive the event again and again. Some children become active for the sake of being active, often bordering on hyperactivity, to distract themselves. And, of course, many have strong beliefs and use traditional religion and prayer as a coping mechanism.

Interviewer: How do children cope with dramatic incidents like bus bombings?

Prof. Lahad: Children have many ways to protect themselves. One is a naïve approach to life. They wish to overcome it and grow up and be normal. Holocaust survivor studies show it is possible to do just this. All people want to survive as human beings. Everyone has a different makeup within them. Life goes on despite terrible incidents or circumstances. They hope that one day there will be peace.

Interviewer: Does the length of the conflict lead to hate or forgiveness?

Prof. Lahad: A personal scar creates problems that are difficult to get over. Parents can help or hurt. But the child will carry the pain within him even if the child decides to come to terms with the enemy. Being exposed to trauma leaves an emotional scar. Some exposed early in life might adopt aggression because they are very young and can't forgive. They have feelings of frustration that they are the recipient of aggression and this can sometimes lead to aggression but not always. It is still not a very clear process.

Interviewer: The recent bus explosion seems to have brought a national grieving to the surface.

Prof. Lahad: Israel is a small country so many people may know someone who is directly affected. There is a very personalized grief tradi-

LEFT: *A friend of the three teenaged girls killed in Tel Aviv speaks at their funeral.*
ABOVE: *A vigil is held for those killed in the Jerusalem bus bombing of February 25, 1996.*

tion in how we react to these events. In Israel we give permission to be sad. You can grieve if something terrible happens.

Interviewer: Israeli children don't seem to know any Arab kids. There seems to be no awareness of each others' lives.

Prof. Lahad: This is very interesting and very strange. It has to do with a defensive wall we all build within us. We live on an imaginary island where the other side doesn't live. When you see them on the road they don't exist for both sides. When a bus blows up all of a sudden they're here. It's a very interesting psychological phenomenon. On one hand it's a healthy sign because it helps both sides to continue living during an active conflict, but over time it becomes a barrier. In a reduced conflict you have to invest in knowing the other side. It once was a defense to say this is not me but the "darkness," the shadow of a monster. So I disengage myself in order to keep my feeling that I'm OK. I'm light and he's all shadow. But for peace to come you have to know the other side and they need to know you. We need to de-stereotype each side if we want to believe both sides are human.

Interviewer: What is unique about Israeli children?

Prof. Lahad: Israeli society is a child-centered society that shelters children even though terrible things happen all around them. We have no child soldiers in Israel. We have "peaceful havens" away from difficult situations. Israeli children are coping well but are not very hopeful about the peace process. The unknown is very frightening. The peace process will cost a lot. Psychologically I won't be in control anymore. After the Rabin assassination more young people looked to peace as a solution. But the reality is more complicated.

One week after the second Jerusalem bus bombing, a twenty-four-year-old Islamic Jihad terrorist from Gaza went to a bustling shopping center in Tel Aviv. He carried on his body twenty kilograms of TNT packed with nails. The terrorist blew himself up as he was crossing a busy street. He killed thirteen Israelis and injured more than a hundred others.

Walking next to him as he crossed the street were three teenage girls out for a day of shopping. Dana was fourteen years old. Hadas was fifteen years old. Bat-Hen was fifteen. It was Bat-Hen's birthday the day she died. The three friends were buried together in side-by-side graves. Their joint headstone read, "In life and death, they did not part."

One of the most difficult events for us to film was the highly emotional funeral of Dana, the last of the teenage girls to be buried the day following the sui-

The family mourns the loss of their daughter Dana.

cide attack. In addition to the rabbi's speech at the funeral, several of the young victims' school friends gave eulogies.

Rabbi: I asked about you and your ways, and I heard you were a flower and a soul loving both man and animal. Your life was cut short by the hands of a demented person who believed that murdering children would be his ticket to paradise. And you, like all of us, believed in loving thy neighbor like thyself.

First Friend: When they asked me to write something about you, I didn't know if I would have the strength. True, we knew that there were terror attacks. We knew that we were not safe. We knew that in every terror attack there are a lot of people who don't come out alive. But we never knew it would happen to us and that it would reach here. All the words that you want to say are simply buried in the tears and in our pain. Dana, if you hear me, we're with you. We're escorting you in your last journey. We will really miss you, the friend we all loved.

Second Friend: I'm sorry this happened. I love you. And Chen [*a nickname for Bat-Hen*] and Hadas and you. They will take care of you. I'm sure they will take care of you. You will be together. You left me here to tell everyone you were good and how you didn't deserve this. I will never forget you. Never. How you laughed that morning and didn't believe you were going to die, Dana. But for me you are still alive in my heart. And so it will always be. I am sorry, Dana. I am sorry.

CLOCKWISE FROM LEFT: *Dana, aged 14, Hadas, aged 15, and Bat-Hen, aged 15, were all killed in the suicide bombing in Tel Aviv on March 4, 1996.*

rwanda

Fifty years after the Holocaust, the world suffered the ravages of another genocide in a small African country. The war in Rwanda is the first genocide officially recognized by the United Nations since the end of World War II.

The mysterious death of President Habyarimana in 1994 was the pretext for Hutu extremists in the Rwandan government to incite mass killings of the Tutsi minority. Habyarimana was a moderate Hutu president who advocated a power-sharing government with the Tutsis. Although never actually proven, it is believed that the president was killed by his own army. Using state-sponsored hate radio, Hutu extremists in the Rwandan government incited the six million Hutu majority to eliminate Rwanda's one million Tutsis, including children. Recordings from the Rwandan Radio Mille Collines broadcast the malevolent message that, "To destroy the big rats, you must kill the little rats," a deliberate reference to targeting the Tutsi children. Along with their parents, these children were the victims of a systematic campaign of extermination.

The Hutu militia, known as the Interahamwe, took to the streets within hours of their president's death. They set up roadblocks to stop and kill Tutsis as they attempted to flee the mass murder. The genocide spread rapidly throughout the country under control of the Hutu-led Rwandan army. The civilian massacres were primitive and performed mostly with clubs and machetes. In just the three months of April, May, and June 1994, eight hundred thousand Tutsi men, women, and children were killed. Three hundred thousand of the dead were children.

Nyamata, south of the capital city of Kigali, was the site of some of the worst acts of genocide during the war. A year after the three-month war ended, the town was still in terrible disarray. Most storefronts were burned-out shells. The town square seemed empty of people. Only a few men, women, and very small children walked the streets. On the outskirts of Nyamata is a mass grave where the remains of an estimated four thousand bodies are buried. Marked only with a simple wooden cross, the mass grave is covered with an enormous mound of red dirt. Bodies had been bulldozed into this large, excavated hole in the ground and then simply covered over.

OPPOSITE: *Rwandan girl in expression therapy, holding bamboo toy rifle.*

ABOVE AND OPPOSITE: *Rwandan children in art therapy class.*

Across the road from this mass gravesite is an elementary school run by the Italian relief organization CUAMM. All the parents of these schoolchildren were murdered during the war and buried in the nearby mass grave. As in Bosnia, Rwandan children are participating in art therapy classes to help them cope with the atrocities they witnessed, but the success of this therapy is very difficult to measure in psychological terms. The extreme trauma the children endured can take control of their lives, causing nightmares and recurring flashbacks of the genocide. Some children also experience an emotional numbing or loss of feelings, a form of self-anesthesia in which intrusive, traumatic experiences are repressed. These boys and girls do not openly exhibit what they are thinking or feeling.

Patrick Kashenshebusca was the teacher in charge of the art therapy class.

Mr. Kashenshebusca: This activity is one of the trauma-healing method-
ologies. It is a practical method for helping children who have witnessed horrible events during the past genocide. One of the ways is
to express the anger, the aggression, the pain they underwent.
Drawing is taken to be very important because it combines three expressions.... It has oral expression because a child is able to talk
about his drawing and at the same time he can write a story on what
he has drawn. So I have found it a very rich technique to help a child
pull out what has been going on in him during the past experience.

Interviewer: Have you noticed a difference in their behaviors since they
started the therapy?

Mr. Kashenshebusca: Oh, yes. There has been a difference because the

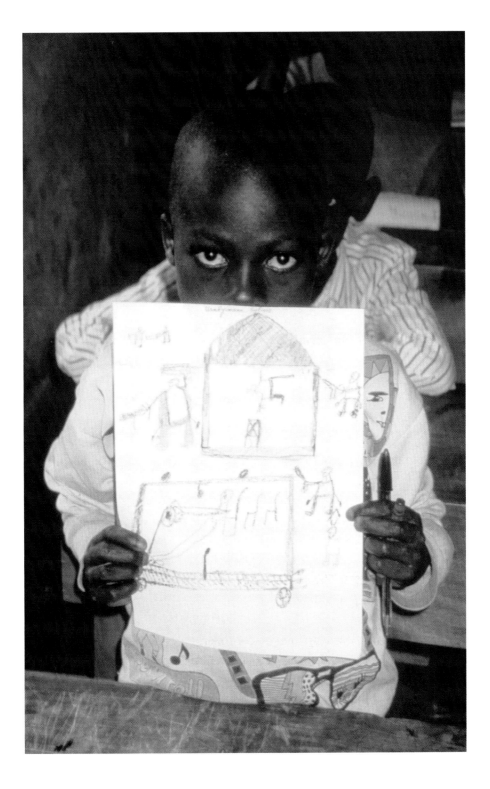

children who have not been able to concentrate in class, or who have been aggressive to other children, or children who have not been associated with others have now come to an almost normal state. Now we note some high degree of concentration, low aggressivity. Fighting among children is not pronounced at all, and also some kind of socialization has improved among children at school.

It also helps the children face the reality because during the war there was a dichotomy between the feelings and the thinking of each other. But now it is facing reality, confronting actually what happened, bringing back the senses to the real thinking of the person and then being able to live with it. It is also seeing reality and being able to cope. In fact, it builds a strong coping mechanism which I think helps a person to live for the future.

The first month we did it several times. We noted improvement among children, those who were unable even to explain their drawings can now start explaining them. Those who were crying all the time are now not usually crying. It depends on what we see, whether there is a slide back or there is progress. And you know, these psychological reactions, we can't easily measure them. Sometimes they may come back. Sometimes the children are really healed, and we don't have to use these psychotherapy methods any longer.

After completing their drawings, several of the children read the stories they had written about the drawings.

Young Girl: [*Describing the drawings on her paper.*] This Interahamwe cut someone with a machete. This Interahamwe has a machete. And they are going to destroy houses and kill people. These are children whose parents have been killed.

This is an Interahamwe chasing a woman who has a child on her back. He tells her, "Stop there. You're about to die." "Have mercy on me," she says. "I won't be a Tutsi again." And the Interahamwe laughs at her. This woman is crying, "He's cutting the child on my back." This child is telling his mother, "Mama, they're going to kill us."

Young Boy: Things happened quickly. One Interahamwe who was our neighbor came and told us that the president had been killed and we would pay for that. We didn't even know that the president had been killed. It was April 7, 1994, in the morning. Nothing happened. The next day, the Interahamwe came with machetes, others with hammers,

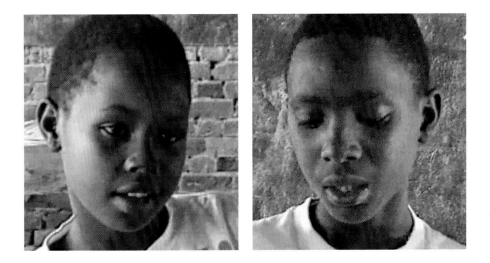

others with small hoes, others with clubs. We started running. The counselor told us to go to the local authority's house. We ran to the place. They wanted us to assemble at the same place in order to kill us there.

Then they came and killed my parents and others who were with us. I managed to hide, and in the evening I went to Nyamata. On my way I met others on the run and we finally arrived. I spent two days at the commune. Then the Interahamwe attacked the Kayumba locality. Soldiers threw grenades while Interahamwe chopped people with machetes. They hit them with clubs. They threw people in holes who were not dead. Those who managed to flee came to the commune, but the Interahamwe attacked us there. The burgomaster and the sous-prefet gave them beer to thank them for their good work.

As for me, I hid in the bush until they discovered me. I ran, and they ran after me, but I managed to outrace them. I finally arrived at the church in Ntarama. I thought I would finally be safe there. At the church I found people detained inside the compound by soldiers. The sous-prefet came and gave the order to kill "those cockroaches." So they chopped us with machetes; I pretended I was dead, and they thought that I was dead.

The next day, three buses full of soldiers arrived. They were going to kill people at Ntarama. They went around singing, "Let's exterminate those cockroaches." I continued to hide among the dead bodies in the church.

Interviewer: What do you think of the people who did the killing?

Young Boy: What I think is that they should be arrested, imprisoned, and punished. I wish there will be no more war in the future so that we

can live together like good neighbors and avoid any other conflict in the future.

This fourteen-year-old boy sought safety in a Roman Catholic church in the nearby town of Ntarama. Like so many others, he believed the house of worship would provide him sanctuary. Instead, he was caught with more than four hundred fleeing Tutsis in a horrific death trap where Hutu militia hacked, clubbed, and shot their trapped victims. The boy survived by lying quietly among the dead bodies for several days.

One year after this massacre, we filmed the same bodies at the Ntarama church. They have been left untouched by the Rwandan government as a memorial to the victims of the genocide, and to ensure that the atrocities of the war are not forgotten. On the floor of the church were shattered, decaying bones, mummified clothing stained with dried blood, and skulls that showed evidence of the machete blows that killed the victims. Their bodies remained in the exact position in which they fell. Skeletons clutching bowls and mattresses were left in running positions. Outside the church, there is a table where many skeletons have been placed, their limbs intertwined. A few yards from the church were smaller buildings where it appears women and children had been hiding. The floor of these buildings is covered in an assortment of children's skulls and skeletons.

There are two such church memorials in Rwanda, the one in Ntarama and another in Nyarubuye. Rwanda is 70 percent Roman Catholic and the church has objected to these memorials. But the fact remains that during the war some priests and church officials collaborated with the Hutu militia, encour-

The skeletal remains of the victims of the genocide are displayed at the Ntarama church memorial.

aging Tutsis to seek shelter in their churches and then leaving them to the killers. In 1998, two Catholic priests were tried and sentenced to death by the Rwandan government for helping orchestrate the genocide.

As the war continued in the spring of 1994, the Rwandan Patriotic Front (RPF), a rebel army of exiled Tutsis from Uganda, invaded the war-torn country. The RPF forces defeated the Hutu militia within three months and drove them out of Rwanda, ending the massacre of Tutsi civilians. During the war, many of the Tutsi children in hiding were picked up by the Rwandan Patriotic Front. These frightened children joined the RPF simply to survive. They were lost, separated from their families, and caught in a combat zone. Many saw their parents killed by the Hutus. The army took the boys in and provided protection, giving them certain duties to perform like cooking and cleaning. But some children as young as ten became soldiers and took part in the fighting. There were approximately twenty-five hundred child soldiers attached to the Rwandan Patriotic Front.

After the war ended, the newly-formed Rwandan government decided to remove these child soldiers from the care of the RPF and establish a center in Butare for demilitarized child soldiers. The center houses several thousand Tutsi boys, seven to seventeen years in age, and provides them with educational and vocational training as a means of reintegrating the boys into society. Hopefully, the schooling will give stability to their lives and help them develop an identity separate from that of a soldier.

We filmed many boys at the center. The first two, Aimable and Jean-Baptiste, were not involved in actual fighting. But the third boy, Jean-Bosco, did participate in combat.

Aimable: When I joined the army I had no clothes and they provided me with new clothes. Since I had not washed myself for a long time, I was very dirty. Because we had spent so much time hiding in the bush, we were so weak. They took care of us.

Demilitarized child soldiers.

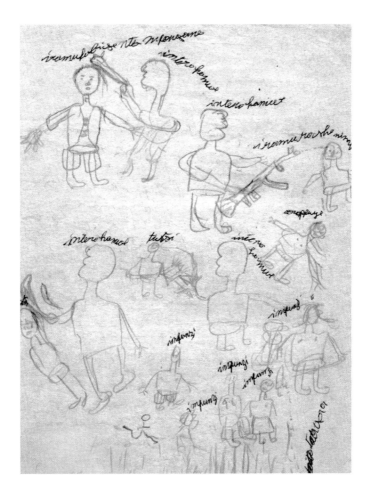

Interviewer: Why did you run to the army? Why didn't you go to a neighbor for help?

Aimable: I didn't go to a neighbor because it was those neighbors who were killing us. I saw that from where I was hiding.

Interviewer: What was it like to travel with the soldiers?

Aimable: I was happy because I wouldn't die. I thought I would die hiding in the bush. I thought the Interahamwe would find me and chop me with machetes. I was just happy to be alive.

Interviewer: How old were you at this time?

Aimable: I was fourteen.

Interviewer: Did you participate in the fighting?

Aimable: I didn't go up to the front line. No. But I watched everything. The RPF kept us safely behind them when they were fighting the enemy. I watched from there.

Interviewer: Do you want to be a soldier?

Aimable: We came here determined to study, so we'll concentrate on studying for now.

Interviewer: Did you witness your parents being killed?

Jean-Baptiste: Yes, I was there when my parents were being killed. Yes.

Interviewer: What happened then?

Jean-Baptiste: When they started killing them, I immediately ran to the bush nearby. From there I watched the killers chop my parents and cut their heads. When I saw that they were dead, I ran away. I had nowhere to go and the Hutu militia wanted to kill me.

Yes I was there when my parents where being killed.

That's when I saw the RPF soldiers and they invited me to stay with them.

Interviewer: What did you do with the soldiers?

Jean-Baptiste: In the military, I used to take care of the soldier's guns. Then I would eat and be happy and wash my clothes. I used to watch how the soldiers would fix their guns.

Interviewer: How old were you when this happened?

Jean-Baptiste: I was eleven years old.

Interviewer: Were there many boys your age fighting with the soldiers?

Jean-Baptiste: Yes, I saw them and I myself could use a gun.

Interviewer: Do you consider yourself a soldier?

Jean-Baptiste: No, I don't consider myself a soldier.

Interviewer: When you grow up, do you want to be a soldier?

Jean-Baptiste: No, because I want to study. It's not time to join the military, so I haven't thought about it. I came here to the center so that I can better serve my country and earn my living.

Although Jean-Baptiste smiled broadly as he proudly stated that he could use a gun, the next boy seemed more defensive than proud of his role as combatant.

Interviewer: What did you do when you were with the soldiers?

Jean-Bosco: I was a fighter.

Interviewer: Did the RPF give you a gun?

Jean-Bosco: Yes, I had a gun.

Interviewer: Do you know if you killed anyone?

I was shooting at my enemy.

Jean-Bosco: I was just fighting. I don't know if I killed anybody. I was shooting at my enemy.

Interviewer: How old were you when that happened?

Jean-Bosco: When I joined the military, I was fourteen years old.

Interviewer: What do you think about the people who caused the war? Did their actions make you angry?

Jean-Bosco: Yes, they made me angry. When we were fighting them, they didn't want to listen. They continued to kill innocent people and molest the population. That made me angry.

Interviewer: What do you think of children fighting alongside adult soldiers?

Jean-Bosco: These children joined the military after their parents were killed. Having nowhere else to go because their neighbors would kill them too, they had no choice but to be soldiers.

Interviewer: Because of this experience of fighting in the war, do you now think of yourself as a man or a boy?

Jean-Bosco: I consider myself a boy.

According to the group Human Rights Watch, Jean-Bosco is one of an estimated 250,000 child soldiers fighting in more than thirty current or recent wars around the world. Although the United Nations Convention on the Rights of the Child expressly prohibits the use of child soldiers under the age of fifteen, government forces or rebel armies in Africa, Asia, and Latin America routinely

interahamwe ituvoka

interahamwe
ibiye kumukubita sitampou
...

Iyo ninterahamwe irigutema umuntu
mu mutwe

interahamwe isandura ama
gura

Bamutemye murjosi arapfa

Abantu bapfuye

interahamwe
aternye
umupfu imay
kuvia

amujjanye mumodoka
ugo babajjane kulata

umukobwa afite egeshwe

interahamwe itema umuntu
akaguru amuvala imbalazi

interahamwe imena
inkono

umukobwa afite inkoko

Mujawira Alex

Mbere mujintambara vari mu Bugande numvaga yuko abantu bapfaga cyane abahutu bica abatutsi babatema badug ~~badug~~ numvaga ko baba bigaga ahantu hose kabe mu mazu no mu rufurzo na handi hose ~

Numvaga ko interahamwe zicaga abatutsi zibatema zibaroba kandi n'umvaga ko ~~bo~~ ho zisenya na maza kandi zikica abantu cyano; cyane mubice by' umugesera ~~+~~ kabandi muyandi ~~jit~~ na ~~ferefe~~ gitura abatutsi ~~bagiys kubohoza~~ ba bohozwe ~~aribace~~ ~~sy~~ kandi bari benshi

n'umvaga ko interahamwe zicaga buri mu tutsi wese kandi zillabica nabi Nko ku juqunyo abantu mu nuzara cyangwa kumutema areba

i Nko muri mizongo ~~47~~ 1994 ha ~~pfuye~~ pfuye abantu benshi cyane

Interahamwe
z'izino guliga
abantu mu rufur~~o~~

INTERAHAMWE
I RASHE UMUNTU

Hutu inmates at the Kigali prison.

enlist boys this young. One reason for the growing use of child soldiers is the availability of modern, lightweight automatic weapons that are simple to operate. The majority of the demobilized Rwandan child soldiers we interviewed for our film did not wish to continue in the military. For them, the war's end was the start of a new life, one that did not include serving again in the army.

One year after the war ended, the newly formed Rwandan government had arrested and jailed 125,000 Hutu men, women, and children accused of participating in the genocide. At the end of 1999, the overwhelmed Rwandan court system has managed to try only a little more than one thousand of these cases. The majority of those found guilty face either the death penalty or life in prison. But for many of the accused Hutu people, life in prison may be inevitable. Guilty or innocent, they will remain imprisoned indefinitely while awaiting trial. This has led to terrible overcrowding and inhumane living conditions for these prisoners.

The Kigali Central Prison is an old structure made of red dirt and cement on the outskirts of the city. Eight thousand inmates are crowded into a space actually built to house only two thousand. There is so little space that most of them must stand. Every inch of floor in the courtyard and inside the prison is occupied by a body. Many of the prisoners wear pink uniforms that seem out of place in this group of vicious murderers. There are no guards in Rwanda's prisons; they are run by the inmates themselves. As we were led around by one of the prisoners, it was difficult not to step on people as they attempted to sleep in any free spots they found. Several prisoners were taking public showers fully clothed.

Separated from the male prisoners is a group of incarcerated women also accused of participating in the genocide. Some of the women inmates had babies sitting on their laps. It is difficult to imagine how they managed to care for these infants in such a setting. The stench of all these people living in such close quarters was overpowering.

While filming, we observed little or no repentance on the part of the accused killers. The Hutu prisoners do not recognize the current Tutsi-led Rwandan government as legitimate, nor do they confess to committing any crimes. Their hope is that the estimated thirty-thousand remaining exiled and armed Hutu guerrillas will attack the prison and liberate them. For these Hutu prisoners, the war continues. In 1997, two hundred Hutu rebels attacked a prison in northwestern Rwanda in an attempt to free their comrades. They managed to release close to a hundred prisoners, though the Hutu rebels suffered heavy casualties from a counterattack by the Rwandan army. Former Hutu soldiers, or militiamen in hiding, continue to be a threat to peace and stability in the region. Without warning, these former members of the Interahamwe routinely attack and kill civilians in the border areas of Rwanda, Congo, and Burundi.

The Kigali Central Prison had housed several hundred Hutu boys under the age of sixteen. In an act seen as unique in modern history, these Hutu boys, some as young as eight to ten years of age, were accused of actively participating in the genocide. Médecins Sans Frontières (Doctors Without Borders) and UNICEF had pressured the Rwandan government to set up a separate secure facility for these accused boys. As a result of this pressure, the Ministry of Justice transferred these child prisoners to a rehabilitation center in Gitagata, a remote rural area south of the city of Kigali.

This juvenile facility, called the Re-education and Production Center, housed 350 Hutu boys drawn from the adult prisons in Rwanda. Their new home was still very grim: a collection of run-down buildings and tents surrounded by a ten-foot high cyclone fence. Some of the boys wore mean, hostile expressions from their year in Kigali Central Prison. Others, however, looked like little kids, who seemed physically incapable of killing anyone. These boys were allegedly recruited into the Hutu youth militias and then armed for the killing of Tutsis. Crispin Sinanyigaya, the director of the Re-education Center, maintains that there is documented evidence that implicates each boy in the killings. Because of their ages, however, these boys will never be brought to trial under Rwandan law. Although 70 percent of the boys

RIGHT: *Rwandan boys accused of participating in the genocide.*

at the Re-education Center can neither read nor write, they receive little or no formal schooling. Instead, they work part of each day as laborers at a nearby farm.

Although most Rwandans believe there was adult complicity in their crimes and that these Hutu boys did not act independently of adults, there is still little sympathy for the boys. The director told us that it would be very difficult to allow these children to go home as they have no community acceptance. Therefore they must remain indefinitely at the Re-education Center. To use the Rwandan government's phrase, "They have been resettled." The center's director also spoke of "morally educating" the boys, of rehabilitating them over a period of years. With some difficulty, we managed to get permission from the Rwandan government to film at the center and to interview a number of boys accused of participating in the genocide. As a way of greeting us, the boys sang a number of Christian songs. The words of one of them were:

> This world that you see, I can't understand it. You who can see better, where is this world going? Keep on fighting the evil, you'll eventually win. Our world is too tempting, but it goes too fast, and eventually evil will be vanquished. Repent today, lean on Jesus, he will fight for us. Keep on fighting, you Christian, you'll eventually win.

The boys sang the songs with high sweet voices and it was hard to imagine them as participants in the genocide. The religious themes they expressed in the song described present despair and evil but looked ahead to a time of triumph

when God rewards those who have fought against sin. The boys must have learned the songs in church, probably long before the genocide took place in their country. Perhaps singing the Christian songs was part of their "moral education"? Obviously it offered some comfort to the boys in coming to terms with their experiences.

After spending time at the Re-education Center and speaking with many of the accused boys, we came away with the clear impression that they all claimed to be innocent of any crimes. It may have been unrealistic to assume the chil-

dren would admit to taking part in the genocide. We first asked them about the conditions they lived in at the Kigali Central Prison.

> **Jean**: It was really bad when I arrived at the Kigali Prison. There were too many people there. I couldn't find a spot to sleep. I had to stand all night and day. Adults would beat us when we tripped on them going to get our food ration.
>
> **Interviewer**: Were you frightened there?
>
> **Jean**: I was very frightened because people were dying of illnesses of all kinds, of dysentery, and I thought that if I caught the illness, I would die too. I am only fifteen years old.
>
> **Interviewer**: Why did they arrest you?
>
> **Jean**: Me? Some woman who came from my region told the police that I was among the killers at the time of the war. She said I killed somebody in the Runda commune in Gitarama prefecture. So they put me in the central prison of Kigali.
>
> **Interviewer**: What do you think of being accused of murder?
>
> **Jean**: Let them investigate my case. I don't even know the person they accused me of killing. I was arrested by someone I don't know. We were about to be interrogated about a theft. They said I was an Interahamwe and that I was a killer. And they don't even say who I killed. I'm innocent. I wish the government would look closer at our cases because I believe most of us in this compound are innocent. And if there are some who did it, they did so because of the orders of adults and authorities.

But many of us here are innocent.

Another boy, Musa, from the Kigali Central Prison told us of his experience.

Musa: I am fifteen years old and I came from Kigali Prison. The prison was terrible. There was no fresh air. There was no room to move about. There was no possibility to play.

Interviewer: How would you compare this place you are in now with the prison?

Musa: It's very different. This place is nice. Here we can play. We have enough space to sleep. We can go to the toilet. We have clean water. We have food.

Interviewer: Why have you been arrested?

Musa: They accused me of beating two people with a stick. They don't say whether those two died. They don't say where those persons are. That's what they accuse me of.

Interviewer: Could you explain it to me because I don't understand? How could the militias make children kill their neighbors?

Musa: What saddens me is that we are in prison now when we are innocent. And those who did the killing, some of them are in prison. But many of us here are innocent. And those who did it, it is because they were forced to do so. You understand that if a grown-up person tells a child like myself to do something, you wouldn't refuse.

Interviewer: What about your future?

Musa: My future? Maybe the time will come and we will be tried and then we'll be able to go home. Those that will be found guilty will be punished accordingly.

The war in Rwanda produced refugee populations of catastrophic proportions. As the Rwandan Patriotic Front declared victory in July 1994, the Hutu militias led a frantic mass exodus from the country. More than one million people fled to Burundi, Tanzania, and Congo, the former Zaire. They settled in huge refugee camps, the largest of which was in the city of Goma on the Rwandan border. Goma is an arid and inhospitable place of volcanic ground barely able to sustain vegetation. The living conditions in the refugee camps were execrable. Makeshift tents provided the only shelter. Food and unpolluted water were scarce or impossible to find. Dehydration and cholera epidemics killed tens of thousands of people a day. For many in the outside world, the heartbreaking photos of the extreme suffering of exiled Rwandans in the refugee camps came to epitomize the Rwandan tragedy and blocked out the horror of the genocide.

The international community, which had refused to make a military intervention in the war, now responded belatedly with emergency relief. The crisis became a humanitarian aid nightmare costing a million dollars a day to support. The refugee camps also provided safe havens for the Hutu militia, the perpetrators of the genocide. Ironically, emergency aid was now being provided to the people who were largely responsible for the war. In fact, these former leaders of the Hutu militia came to control the refugee camps and in the process intimidated those who wished to return home.

Among the other refugees in the camps were an estimated 114,000 "lost children of Rwanda." These children were orphaned, abandoned, or separated from their families during the genocide and panicked migration. They suffered high mortality rates in the camps from cholera and malnutrition. They were the youngest casualties of the war.

An ambitious tracing program was launched by a number of aid groups working together to reunite these lost children with their relatives. The International Red Cross, Save the Children, and UNICEF devised an innovative photo identification project that registered the images of over twenty thousand unaccompanied children. The simple photographs showed the lost children holding boards imprinted with a numerical code for identification purposes. These pictures were then posted on billboards around the refugee camps. More copies of the photos were taken to villages in Rwanda in the hope that people there could identify the children. Using these pictures, as well as basic information provided by the children, aid workers began the daunting task of reuniting the children with their families.

In one of the few happy endings to the war, humanitarian aid organizations worked together to reunite thirty-three thousand lost children with their families. The majority of these children had been separated for more than one year.

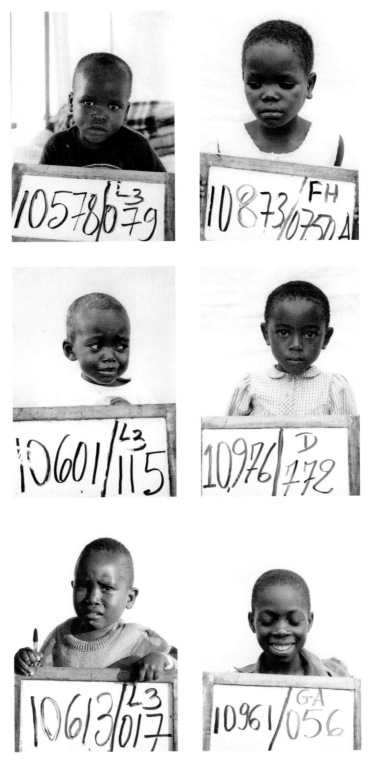

ID photos of some of the lost children of Rwanda.

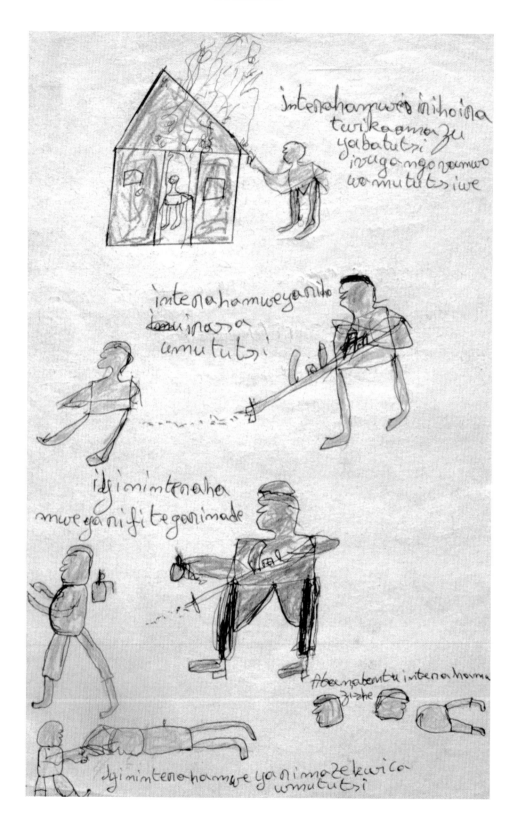

A mother is reunited with her lost children.

We filmed one such emotional reunion in Kigali when the International Red Cross returned children from the refugee camps in Goma. As the jeeps and minibuses drove up the dirt driveway, the waiting parents, relatives, and siblings of the exiled children ran to see who had returned. On the day we filmed, nineteen children came home. They embraced and hugged each other. Many parents and children cried. Some children looked stunned that they were safely back in Rwanda.

Father: [*Referring to his little boy.*] Yes, he recognized me, but he cried a lot. When he saw me, he started crying. A whole year is a lot of time.
Interviewer: Is this a reunited family?
Mother: Yes, she is my child. She disappeared during the war in April. This month she is fifteen years old. She's thin, but I'm glad to see her whatever she looks like. There's one more we lost but he didn't go outside. He must be inside Rwanda. I lost him before the war. I publicized his name but they have not found him yet. I believe he is in Rwanda. He's small. He's only eight years old.

We asked the International Red Cross worker who had driven the children home that day to describe the process of reunification.

Red Cross Worker: Just after the war we started to register all the unaccompanied children in a database. We have now seventy thousand
children registered in our database. So when the parents come to us,
we look for their child. We look in the database and very often we
can locate the child. So after this we put them in contact through
messages, and if both agree, we make the family reunion.

Interviewer: And what was the purpose of taking the Polaroid pictures
today of the children hugging their parents?

Red Cross Worker: Because in Zaire unfortunately there are a lot of rumors
about what happens in Rwanda, and a lot of children are afraid to
come back to Rwanda. They think they won't be really reunited with
their family. So when they find their parents, we take a picture and we
send it to Zaire so that the people in Zaire can see that the child was really reunited with his family. Some people say that the family reunions
are a trick, and that children won't be reunited to their families. So to
try to gain the confidence of everybody, when the family reunion is
done, we show the picture of the child and his parent and we send it to
Zaire to prove that the family reunion was really done.

Interviewer: Was today a good day?

Red Cross Worker: Yeah, it was quite a good day because very often
some children, they change their mind at the last minute and just the
morning before the family reunion they say, "No, I won't go back to
Rwanda." And today it didn't happen. We're quite happy.

But for many unaccompanied children, there is no family to go home to.
The war left tens of thousands of children living on their own and struggling
to survive.

Many of these children also have had to become the guardians of their
younger siblings.

Other lost children have been placed in eighty different orphanages in
Rwanda where they may spend their entire childhood. The SOS Center in Kigali, also known as the Village d'Enfants, is an Austrian-run orphanage. Two of
the girls we interviewed there are Murekatete and Uwamuhoza. Both children
appeared to be deeply traumatized by their war experiences. Murekatete is
twelve years old. While hiding in the bush, Murekatete witnessed the Interahamwe killing her older sister and her sister's children.

Murekatete: Two men came to our house while we were playing with
other children, and they asked me where my older sister was. They

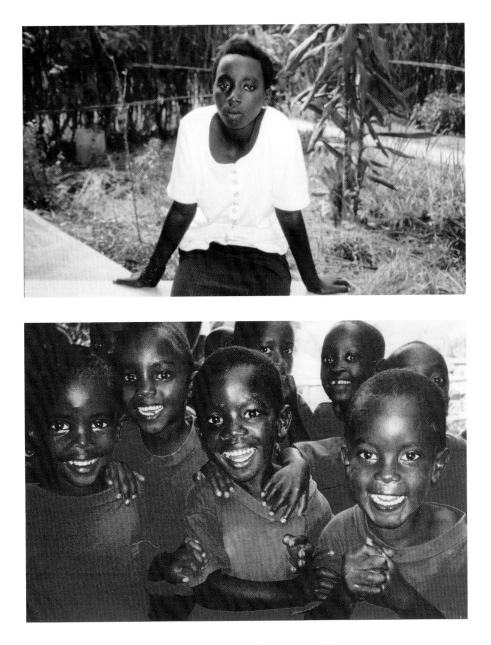

ABOVE, TOP: *Murekatete, age 12.*

ABOVE, BOTTOM: *Orphaned children at the SOS Center, Kigali.*

said that they knew we were Tutsi and that they were looking for my older sister. I went and told my older sister that men were looking for her. My sister told me, "I can't hide with my children because they cry anyway, so find a hiding place, and I'll tell them that I sent you on an errand."

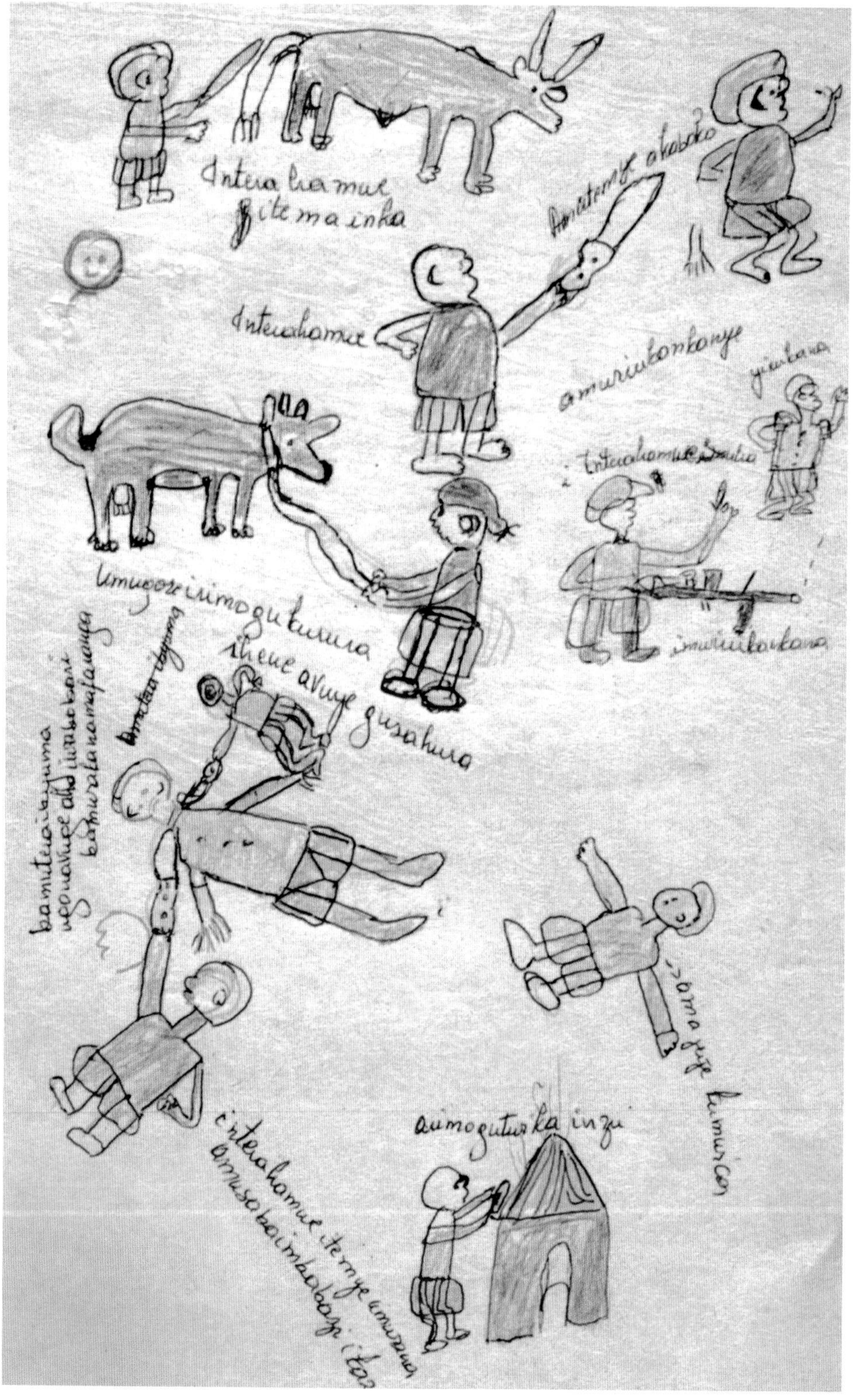

I went behind the compound and put on old clothes we had around the compound and then I hid myself. Then they took my older sister and her children. They tied the children's arms on their backs and did the same to my older sister, they tied the children together, and they kicked my sister telling her that she was a Tutsi, that she had no place in Rwanda, and they could burn her alive. They dragged her out of the compound, and other people began looting the house. They cut one of her children on the neck with a knife.

My sister pleaded with them to let her children alone and kill her instead. They said they couldn't have mercy for a cruel person. She asked them what evil she had done to them. They said because she was a Tutsi, she was one of them. And if she didn't show them where her younger sister (myself) was, she would die a very cruel death, that she would also die for me. She told them again, "I sent my sister on an errand, maybe she met with others and they killed her?" Then they hit her so hard that she fell down on her back. Then they plunged a knife in her belly. She cried a lot, her bowels came out, and they took one of her children who was crying a lot and calling "Mother! Mother!"; they cut him and put him on top of his mother and chopped both with machetes. I wanted to join them but my sister, who was about to die, made a secret sign to me to get away.

I ran away and hid in the bush, meeting others who were also on the run. We tried to seek safety but instead reached a roadblock manned by Interahamwe. They asked us why we were fleeing. They said that maybe we were Tutsi. They pulled our noses. Then they asked me where I came from. I told them. I was trembling with fear. After they pulled my nose they told me that they would kill me last as a dessert. [*Members of the Tutsi population were believed to have more "European" facial features than the Hutu. Consequently one test of whether or not someone was a Tutsi was to measure their noses and other features.*]

One of the women the Interahamwe had also stopped at the roadblock was pregnant. They told her that she was pregnant with a Tutsi child, a viper. They put her on the ground and opened her belly. They took the child out, and the bowels came out too. The small child they had taken out of her womb was moving, and they cut it with a knife and put it on the top of the dying mother. After seeing that, they made me and another woman sit at the roadblock for five days. For five days we sat there with no food or water, thinking at any moment they would kill us. Finally the Interahamwe let us go. I don't know why they didn't kill us. We again ran into the bush. More Hutu soldiers continued to search for us and shot their rifles into the bush where we were, but by chance no bullets touched us. So we stayed in that bush until the night—we ate uncooked corn because we had no other food. When we reached fields, we would take ears of corn and eat them uncooked.

When we left our place of hiding, we continued to walk in the forest of Kicukiro, and we met people who had military uniforms on. We were overtaken by fear thinking that they too were Interahamwe. We told them where we were going and our whole story. We thought they were going to kill us. We thought that this was the end of our lives. They told us that they were Inkotanyi. [*This is another name for the Rwandan Patriotic Front.*] We were happy to hear that.

They hid us in the bush and went to fight and they would bring us food, we were three of us, and the RPF would continue fighting. Others came and asked us where we were going and we told them and they continued to hide us as they fought.

Interviewer: Do you feel safe now?

Murekatete: My heart will never be at peace again because I saw too many things.... I don't know....

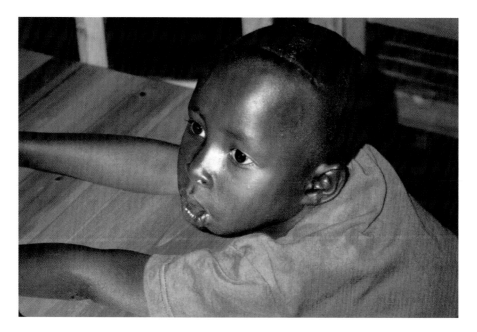

Uwamuhoza, age 5.

Uwamuhoza is a five-year-old girl who was found lying next to her murdered parents. She suffered three machete blows to her head and face, and was left to die. The scars on her head, though quite visible, have healed now. The emotional scars this little girl suffered may never heal.

Interviewer: Can you tell us how you got hurt?

Uwamuhoza: It's the Hutu. It's the Hutu.

Interviewer: Can you describe how it happened?

Uwamuhoza: We were hiding. My dad, my mom, and myself. And they came and killed us. They cut me with a machete and killed me. I was running with my mother and my dad. They saw us and they came and killed us.

Interviewer: Why do you think they did it?

Uwamuhoza: They did it for nothing.

In addition to art therapy, social workers and psychological counselors in Rwanda use a healing technique known as "expression therapy." In expression therapy, Rwandan children re-enact the genocide, some playing the part of its victims, others playing Hutu militia or RPF soldiers. Leanne McCowan, a therapist working for Compassion International, an Australian relief agency, uses expression therapy, or playacting, in a Rwandan orphanage supported by the group.

Rwandan children participating in expression therapy holding toy bamboo guns.

Leanne McCowan: The main aim is to help children to express what they witnessed as a way of treatment, to help them to recover from their trauma. And for children the best way to do it is through drama and singing, drawing—ways to get them to initiate discussion and to start to express what happened to them.

The children created the whole play themselves. At the beginning of the week, we broke them into discussion groups, about five children in each group to discuss their experience during the war. And then after they had done that, we asked them to create a drama based on their experience. So the children created the whole program themselves. Everything that was in the play was something that these children had seen and witnessed during the war.

At the beginning of the week, there were tears, especially in the discussion groups when they were discussing their individual experiences and sharing those experiences. And the aim of the week was for them to be able to express and to get all the emotion out. And eventually by the end of the week, they were able to present the drama without the intense emotion.

The main treatment for healing trauma is expression. They need to be able to retell their story enough times so that they have control over what happened to them rather than have their experience controlling them. So the aim of this whole week was to express what happened through talking, drama, drawing, and singing.

Interviewer: What roles do they decide to take? Do they take roles as literally what happened to them or their parents? Or do they take different roles?

Leanne McCowan: I think that for most of the children there was a mixture of some taking on roles they had witnessed happening to family members or roles they were involved with themselves. Some children chose to be RPF soldiers, some chose to be Hutu militia. The reason that children choose various roles will vary. Some children take roles they were in themselves, whereas other children take on roles they wish they had played. So if they wish they had saved their brother or their parents, they may take on that role in the drama or they may take on an RPF role of coming and saving people.

For some children, they may take on the role of the Hutu militia as a way of letting out their anger and perhaps getting some revenge. The children here were from all different areas within the country. Some of their families were killed during the war; some of their fam-

ilies have fled from the country, so they aren't sure where their families are. Some were victims, and some were also involved in the killings. So there is a whole mixture of children within the orphanage.

Interviewer: So you have both Hutu and Tutsi children here?

Leanne McCowan: Yes.

Interviewer: And how are the children getting along?

Leanne McCowan: I think the children are relating fairly well together. They have normal childish thoughts. But I think there doesn't seem to be any major conflicts between the two ethnic groups within the orphanage.

Interviewer: And what happens to children who don't have therapy like this, who don't have an opportunity to act out or draw picture?

Leanne McCowan: A lot of the trauma research is showing that people who don't have this opportunity can live with their trauma for the whole period of their life. They're doing research on people from World War II, who were children in that period. They are now receiving help as adults, and therapists are seeing big changes in their life. So what actually happens with trauma is that it takes control. Children may have flashbacks throughout the day where they suddenly believe they are back in the war. They have nightmares. A whole range of things can happen to them when they don't have control. So the aim of the treatment is not to make them forget but to give them some control. So when they remember, it is not with the anxious intensity of feeling, and they have more control of what they remember so it doesn't just suddenly come back to them.

Interviewer: How did you happen to come across such a broad section of both Hutu and Tutsi children?

Leanne McCowan: These children were brought to the orphanage by various people. A lot of them were picked up along the road or found hiding in the bushes, and they were brought here by other citizens as well as soldiers. So it wasn't any choice as to which children came here. It was just whatever children were brought here.

Interviewer: And did their parents participate in the killings?

Worker: For some of the children, they did, and for some of those children their parents may have fled or they may have been killed as well. So for a lot of those children, they're dealing with issues of guilt.

Rwandan children have survived this horrific war through astonishing resourcefulness and great good fortune. Most of the children we met had wit-

nessed the brutal killing of their parents or family. They had all instinctively run away and hid from their aggressors. They then were set on a journey of survival to find safety, shelter, or food. They demonstrated the kind of courage under fire that you would think only soldiers would have to produce.

The playacting that the children performed was an emotional and dramatic display of what they had witnessed: people huddled in a church begging for their lives; a woman with a baby on her back busy slitting throats and stealing clothes from dead bodies; soldiers marching in perfect order arriving to save them; medical workers helping the injured. It was a scene of chaos with screaming and crying. It was also an exercise the children were proud to perform.

The children then gathered together and sang, with the most angelic voices, the following song:

> All you visitors here present, let us tell you about this war.
> We lost our parents. They killed our relatives, they de-
> stroyed our homes, they made us suffer, they tortured us
> when we were innocent.
> You can't understand how we managed to survive.
> We survived the machetes,
> you can't understand how we managed to survive.
> They killed our relatives, they destroyed our homes, they
> will answer to that.

We hid in the bush. They saw us and badly beat us. Where
there were places of worship, the killers turned the places
into rivers of blood.
We survived, we survived from among the machetes,
you can't understand how we managed to survive.
You can't understand how the orphans who survived machete blows managed to survive.
The babies who survived from among the machetes,
you can't understand how they managed to survive.
The good friends who survived machete blows,
you can't understand how we managed to survive.
We survived, we survived from the machetes,
you can't understand how we managed to survive.

In addition to singing the song, a young girl named Marie-Rose read the following poem she had written:

War broke out in Rwanda on April 6, 1994. The death
of the Invincible (President Habyarimana) provided the
pretext. The bad people looted and killed at will. Those
cruel men deprived Rwanda of its population, be it children, be it old men, be it women, be it men, be it young
girls and boys, even fetuses in wombs were not spared.
There were tears and sobs of unutterable cruelty. You

would hear noises everywhere, and where you were hiding in the bush, you could see rivers of blood, and fear would dislodge you from the refuge, and then you were badly beaten to death.

Those who were your friends and with whom you used to share everything would chase you with clubs in order to kill you as if you had stolen anything from them. What was even sadder was to see a parent who had children and thus knew the pains of raising a child, dare kill a baby.

A wise Rwandan once said that "all hearts were not given equal qualities," then came benefactors, those are the Rwandan Patriotic Front soldiers, who picked us from the bush and the swamp and brought us together.

Youth, you the Rwanda of tomorrow, war destroys and does not build, I hope you all saw that.

You youth, you the future of Rwanda, I'm asking you to show wisdom, restraint, and respect, because the good future of Rwanda depends on us. Perhaps our Rwanda will return to normal one day.

And you visitors, you parents, and you youth the future of Rwanda, we didn't think that our country would have order again, that's why we continue to thank God who protected us up to this day.

northern ireland

The children of Northern Ireland have suffered terribly during the "Troubles," growing up in a society where terrorism and violence have created a constant climate of fear. Three generations of Northern Ireland's children have never known a permanent peace. Many innocent children have died. Some were killed with plastic bullets fired by British security forces. Others were blown up in Irish Republican Army (IRA) bombings. Some were shot by masked gunmen from Protestant paramilitary groups. All were victims of the inter-connection of religion and politics and were witnesses to one of the twentieth century's most unyielding hostilities.

The "Troubles" in Northern Ireland began in 1969 when the Catholic minority population of the British province started a civil rights protest demanding equal status in jobs, housing, and government. These demands for social justice were accompanied by widespread civil disobedience, and led the British security forces to use repressive measures to restore order. Events such as "Bloody Sunday" in 1972, in which fourteen unarmed Catholic demonstrators were killed by British Army paratroopers, deepened the sectarian divide between the majority Protestant population that wished to remain part of the United Kingdom and the minority Catholic population that wanted a united Ireland free of British control.

As resentment and distrust of the British government deepened among Northern Ireland's Catholics, the Irish Republican Army, which had been dormant for many years, began a terrorist campaign of shootings and bombings largely directed at British security forces. This escalated Britain's attempt to quell the unrest. They sent thousands of troops to Northern Ireland to combat the IRA and both sides soon found themselves enmeshed in an intractable low-intensity war of terrorism that has lasted three decades. This legacy of violence has claimed more than thirty-two hundred lives, half of them in the city of Belfast. Outlawed Protestant paramilitary groups such as the Ulster Defense Force emerged in the 1980s and began their own terrorist campaign of ran-

OPPOSITE: *Republican mural in Derry, Northern Ireland.*

117

domly killing Catholics. Northern Ireland degenerated into a society where terrorism and the political fringe controlled life in the province.

Recent events in Northern Ireland point to a possible end to the "Troubles" and a return to normal life in the province. On April 10, 1998, a 70 percent majority of the people in Northern Ireland voted for the landmark Good Friday Peace Accord. The peace plan seeks to redress the political imbalance in Northern Ireland. It will create a series of power-sharing institutions among the Catholic minority political parties known as Republicans and the majority Protestant parties known as Unionists. However, the Good Friday Peace Accord is a promise, not a guarantee, of a peaceful future for Northern Ireland. In the nineteen months since it was voted upon, the Peace Accord has yet to be implemented. The breakdown of the peace plan stems largely from Unionist demands for the start of a weapons handover, or de-commissioning, from the IRA. Since the IRA has refused to do this, the Good Friday Peace Accord is stalled, with the grave possibility that it may yet end in failure.

Our documentary was filmed in the optimistic period during which the Peace Accord was being drafted. We therefore thought it appropriate to focus, in part, on one of the most positive aspects of Northern Ireland society—its integrated schools. Started in the early 1980s by a grassroots parents movement to bring their children together, these integrated schools are a real alternative to the existing segregated school system in Northern Ireland. Most boys and girls go to either a Protestant or a Catholic school. Integrated schools enroll students of equal numbers from

LEFT: *Catholic children standing in front of a Republican mural.*

Loyalist mural.

both the Catholic and Protestant communities. These schools were opposed by the Catholic church and not supported by the British government. Only 5 per-cent of Northern Ireland children attend integrated schools, but their impor-tance is symbolic for it demonstrates that the two groups can peacefully co-exist. Today there are over thirty integrated schools in Northern Ireland.

One of the first was the Forge Integrated Primary School established in 1985 in Belfast. We filmed at the school and asked a class of eleven-year-old boys and girls to write an essay for us concerning the "Troubles" in Northern Ireland. Once again the children's insights into the politics of their country are poignant and they all seem to have a hopeful belief in their country's future.

MY VIEWS ON THE TROUBLES
by Rory Sweeney

When I was born, there had been violence between Loyalists and Republicans for fifteen years. In 1969, the Troubles started. I don't know much about what happened in the first years, but I assume it was much the same as now or as it used to be, shootings and bombings and such. I have clear memories of some scenes of places where people have been killed, like in 1993 when the UVF killed two people outside a bookmaker's down the Ormeau Road. I remember going past in the car and seeing flowers outside the

Children from Forge Integrated Primary School.

shop. I can also remember the bomb on the Shankill Road which left ten people dead. I can remember the face of the man who planted it. In 1994 a ceasefire was called. We thought this would be the end to the Troubles and I remember the shock when the Canary Wharf bomb went off, and the IRA said they were further away from a second ceasefire than ever.

CONFLICT IN NORTHERN IRELAND
by Eve B.

The Troubles in Northern Ireland have affected everyone, mainly the people who have had family or friends or themselves scarred for life. When the ceasefire was broken, I felt deeply disappointed. I truly thought that peace would last and there wouldn't be any more killings or bombings. I thought wrong. The IRA have started fighting again, though it is not as bad as before. There aren't as many bombings and shootings, but it is still fighting, and we still don't have peace throughout Northern Ireland. There have been many protests for peace and for the IRA and other terrorist groups to make a ceasefire. My only hope is that we do make peace once again and Belfast will be a happy place to live and grow up. Then I will be able to say that I come from Northern Ireland without feeling embarrassed and ashamed.

THE TROUBLES

by Rian

For the last twenty-five years, people have been fighting a pointless war. There is no good reason to kill. Separating families nearly for life because of single actions. Killing and hurting people. Never trying to sit down and discuss the matter. Seeing what the problems are. There's always a better way to solve things rather than killing. It is sad the humans can't work together, discuss the matter. They just go for the easy option. What have the terrorist groups obtained from twenty-five horrible years of killings and beatings? Nothing.

CONFLICT IN N.I.

by Sally

I think the conflict in N.I. is pointless, but on the other hand I think it's good that people are sticking for what they believe in, but this isn't the way to go about it.

I am agnostic but I still think Ireland should be kept apart from the UK so we can be unique and independent by ourselves. It is possible that the talks will come to some sort of an agreement, though it won't suit everyone. It will still stop some of the violence. In my whole life, I have never known peace and it

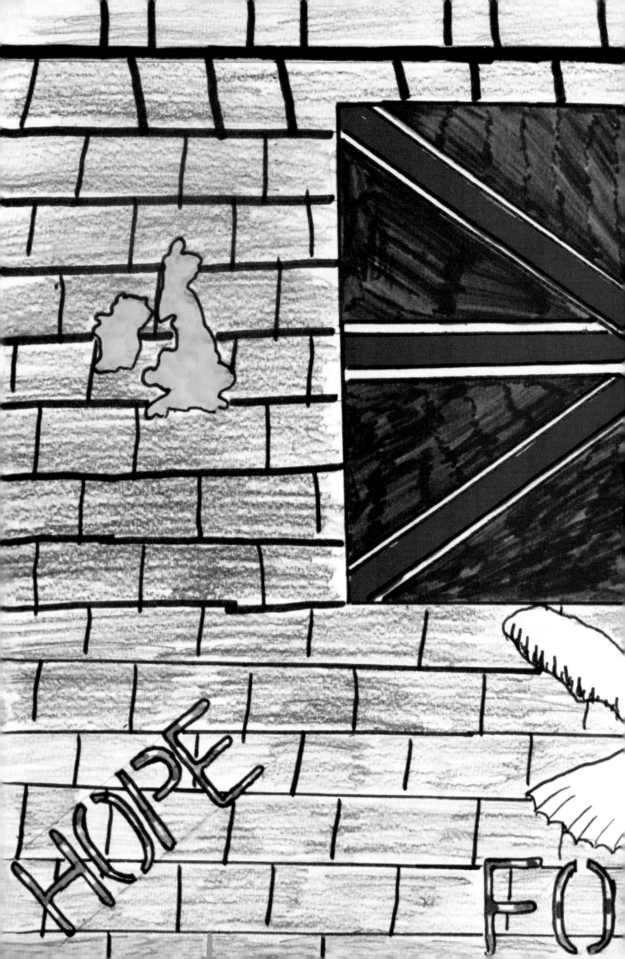

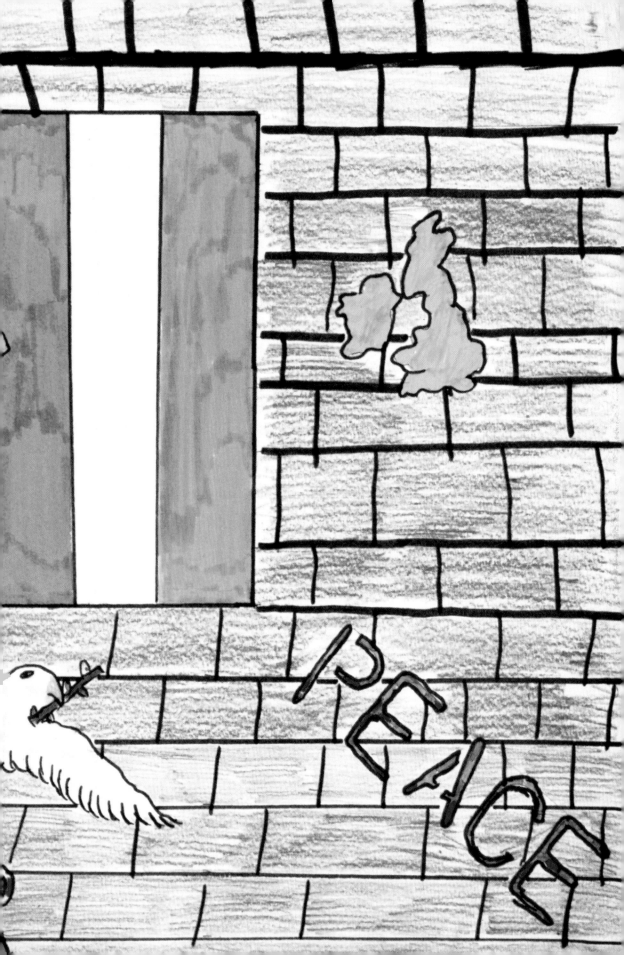

would be good to know complete peace, not having to walk past vandalism on the walls and when people ask me where I come from, I will be proud to say Northern Ireland, because then and only then would we have achieved lasting peace.

MY VIEWS ON THE TROUBLES
by Stuart

Before the ceasefire, things were really bad. I can remember when I was seven years old I was with my mum in town, and I and everyone in the street heard gunshots. An orange car went past going really fast and a police car followed behind. My mum had to stand in front of me so that I wouldn't be shot. And on the news there was always bombs going off and how one man was shot dead and another injured, or one man been hit round the head with a iron bar.

There was even an explosion right in front of Miss Hagerty's house. It turned out there was a bomb. I just wish it would stop and that's going to happen when both sides trust each other to lay down their arms and talk. I just wish there was no troubles.

CONFLICT IN NORTHERN IRELAND
by Mark

I think the conflict in Northern Ireland is a disgrace. Why can't Catholics and Protestants be friends like they are in our school?

And why troubles over whether Northern Ireland should be part of Britain? Why don't people talk and agree? If the leader won't talk for your country, then we should elect a leader who will talk.

The only things that are different between Catholics and Protestants is they have different beliefs and why should beliefs cause troubles?

MY VIEWS OF THE TROUBLES
by Cathy

After twenty-five years of violence, there was a ceasefire in Northern Ireland in the year 1994. People were happy to know their children were going to grow up in peace without fighting or killing. People were happy to know that they could walk down a street without the fear of being shot or hurt by a bomb. But then

Patricia, age 15.

in January of 1996, there was an announcement that the IRA had renewed the violence. People were upset and angry. All these promises had been broken. After seventeen months of peace, the killing began again. At the moment, talks are being held to try to bring the peace back to Ireland so we could live in a world without violence. I used to be frightened every night before the ceasefire that the IRA would come to my house and I would lose my Mum and Dad. So now I don't know if I could stand another broken ceasefire.

MY VIEWS OF THE TROUBLES
by Jade

I have only had one experience of the Troubles, and that was in my old street. We were suspected of having illegal guns in our house. Even though it wasn't us, they later found out it was the people next door. They got arrested and moved to England. Part of the reason we moved was to do with the Troubles in our area. Where I live now is much more peaceful but I'm afraid it might not be so peaceful if the Troubles continue. There is always someone fighting with someone else because of their religion. I wish there was peace and I'm sure a lot of other people feel the same way.

In Belfast, one of the most striking symbols of the deep divide between Catholics and Protestants are the eighteen-foot-high walls known as "Peace Lines" that separate Catholic and Protestant neighborhoods. What started in 1969 as makeshift, temporary barricades of sandbags and wire are now permanent structures of concrete, steel bars, bricks, and corrugated iron. The walls foster the sectarian geography of Belfast and are the symbols that the two communities cannot live together in peace. There are thirty such peace walls in the city and more are being built.

Patricia is a fifteen-year-old girl who lives next to a large red brick peace wall in a Catholic neighborhood known as the Short Strand.

Patricia: Just behind my house here is my local church. I go there every week. Over this way is a Protestant area just across the road behind the bushes. The two communities are very close, so they are. And those houses are a Protestant area. Just those flats in there. All these house are a Protestant area too. They've got those railings up to

A Peace Line wall in Belfast.

keep the two communities apart. Not that it's worked that much. The neighborhood is mainly all Catholic. It's pretty small and near the center of the city in Belfast.

I do feel that people are very unfortunate not to be able to go into each other's communities without any hassle. I would wonder a lot what their streets would be like? Would they be the same as the streets in the Short Strand? I would love to go into a Protestant area. Have Protestant friends. Go out with Protestant friends. When I'm older, go for a drink with Protestant friends. It's very hard when you're split up in your different communities, and you don't want to know each other and that sort of thing.

I do feel a bit sad about what's happened to my childhood. I haven't actually had a very normal life where I can go out into the street, go into different communities and they wouldn't say a word to me. But unfortunately, it's not like that at all now. And it never really will be, I don't think.

I don't really think I would like to settle down here because I don't think there is going to be any peace. I wouldn't want my children growing up in what I knew. You know: the bombs, fighting, what happened in the past and why it is. Things like that. I would try and keep my children away from that as much as possible. Have a normal life for them, a comfortable life.

After all this, I don't think one side is going to back down.

Bonfires in Belfast celebrate the Orange Order during "The Marching Season."

They're too strong. The IRA and the UVF are not going to back down. They would feel they were surrendering or giving in if they make the smallest move of handing in their firearms.

I don't think there will be peace.

The sectarian divide in Northern Ireland is further reinforced each summer in what is known as "the Marching Season." During June, July, and August more than two thousand Orange Order parades are held. Orangemen are a pro-British Protestant fraternal order that celebrates the Protestant triumph over Irish Catholics three hundred years ago, when William of Orange defeated his Catholic father-in-law King James II in the Battle of the Boyne. The

Protestant parades often spark conflict due to their defiant routing through Catholic neighborhoods.

In 1996, the British government banned the Drumcree Parade in County Armagh, the birthplace of the Orange Order. The parade route was redirected and its marchers were prevented from walking through a small Catholic neighborhood along the Garvaghy Road into Portadown. This re-routing of the Orangemen parade provoked four nights of violent protests by Protestants demanding their right to march. The police fired more than five hundred rounds of plastic bullets at the demonstrators who hurled petrol bombs, iron bars, and other missiles at the security forces. These violent Protestant protests were the worst in Northern Ireland in twenty years.

This widespread chaos and disorder forced the British government to reverse its ban on the Orange Order Parade. This resulted in Catholic demonstrators trying to block the parade's route along the Garvaghy Road with a sit-down protest. The Royal Ulster Constabulary (RUC), Northern Ireland's 90 percent Protestant police force, clubbed the demonstrators and forcefully removed them from blocking the parade. Catholic opponents of the march felt betrayed by the British government. This parade and others like it are perceived as a triumphant expression of Protestant domination over their Catholic neighbors.

Karen is a seventeen-year-old girl whose father is a convicted IRA bomber,

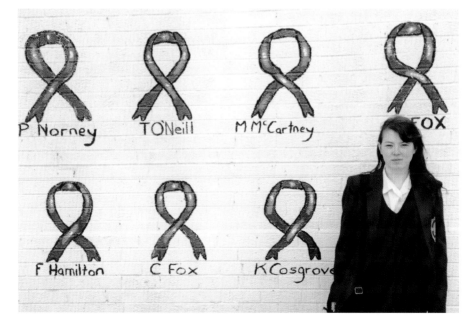

Karen, age 17. OPPOSITE: *Karen with neighborhood children.*

one of the "hard men" who fought against British control of Northern Ireland. Karen lives in West Belfast, off the Falls Road, a strong Republican neighborhood. Wall murals in this exclusively Catholic area display such sentiments as: "There Was No Famine," "Twenty-five years of Resistance and 25 More If Needs Be," "Brits Out!," "Disband the RUC," and "Stop the Torture of Irish POWs in English Jails." We walked home from school with Karen and stopped in front of a wall mural for the group Saoirse, an IRA prisoner's rights group. The wall showed many green ribbons, each with a name painted under it.

Karen: These are green ribbons, a campaign started up by the group Saoirse to release all political prisoners in Ireland. And also the Irish prisoners in England and other places throughout the world. This is part of it. This again is the Saoirse mural. And in this particular area there are fourteen prisoners of war.

Interviewer: Show me which one you made.

Karen: Well, I helped paint all of them but this was the first one I done because it's my father and he's in jail.

Interviewer: Has your father been accused of being a terrorist?

Karen: By the British army and the RUC. Yes. He has been accused of being a terrorist. Although as the saying goes, one man's terrorist is another man's freedom fighter.

I don't consider myself to be "Northern" Irish or living in "Northern" Ireland. I consider myself to be Irish and living in Ireland. And as a Republican, I don't recognize the border. And for me and my older brother it was really hard because we understood that he was being jailed for things that we didn't see as crimes. Because he was standing up for something he believed in.

Interviewer: He was accused of making a bomb and having explosives?

Karen: There was no explosives found. He was charged basically with having what they say was components to make a bomb. But basically it was things you would find in any normal household.

Interviewer: And how long has he been in prison?

Karen: Well, it will be four years this summer. He was sentenced to ten years but with the introduction of remission, 50 percent remission, he's to serve five. This photograph is of me and my daddy and my brothers and sisters. It was took up at the jail Long Kesh. [*IRA prisoners refer to the Maze prison as Long Kesh.*]

There was no substantial evidence but the RUC, the so-called police force which we refuse to recognize, they made up a charge that day. They made up a whole new charge just to get him in prison as they've done with so many people because they couldn't beat a confession out of him. They just charged him with whatever they wanted.

And I just take it that it has to happen because they're fighting for a cause. And although there has been bombs and things in this area and there's been assassinations from Loyalists. And during the summer, the twelfth of July, there's petrol bomb attacks and things. But to me that's just the way it has to be. Because the Irish Republican Army are fighting for a cause that I believe in and many other people believe in as well.

Karen: In Saint James' there's a lot of streets and it's all Catholic.

Interviewer: And does everyone in this neighborhood share the same political views?

Karen: Well, no. I wouldn't say everybody shared the same political views, although they're all Catholic and the majority are Nationalists. They all don't believe in what the IRA are doing. And just across the road...across the main road there is what we call "the village" and that's all Protestant. And then during the summer there's usually a lot of stone throwing between both areas, Catholics and Protestants.

Interviewer: So it's very close?

David, age 11.

Karen: Yeah. It's just maybe five minutes if you walk around the corner.

Interviewer: And do you ever go over there?

Karen: No. It would be too dangerous. There would always be a chance of maybe somebody finding out that you're a Catholic. And then you could get serious beatings, maybe even killed. Just around the corner there's two shopping centers that's shared by both Catholics and Protestants.

Interviewer: So you sometimes see a Protestant?

Karen: Yeah. Although you can't actually tell whether or not they're a Protestant.

If the Falls Road in Belfast represents the heart of the Catholic community, then the Shankill Road is the hub of its Protestant community. Up and down the Shankill Road there are numerous wall murals celebrating this culture. Signs such as "Welcome to the Loyalist Heartland of Ulster," "No Surrender," "We Will Never Accept a United Ireland," and "One Ulster, One People, One Faith, One Crown" greet visitors to the area. In addition to these slogans, there are other, more sinister, murals depicting men in black hoods wielding automatic rifles. These murals are demonstrations of the alleged strength of outlawed Protestant paramilitary groups such as the Ulster Volunteer Force (UVF) or the Ulster Freedom Fighters (UFF). Many also incorporate the symbol of Ulster, the Red Hand.

David, an eleven-year-old boy, explained one such painting of a red hand surrounded by the words "Release the UVF Prisoners." David's father is a member of the Ulster Volunteer Force, a group known for their random murdering of Catholics as revenge for IRA violence. David's father is serving time in the Maze, Northern Ireland's maximum security prison in Lisburne just outside of Belfast. The HM Prison Maze, as it is officially known, is Europe's largest prison and houses more than five hundred IRA and Protestant terrorists in separate quarters.

Interviewer: David, tell us what is this sign about.

David: It's for the release of the prisoners, so it is. It's to stop war. It's to stop all the war from going on and let the prisoners out.

Interviewer: Will this include your dad?

David: It includes all the daddies, so it does.

Interviewer: Well, it says to release the UVF prisoners.

David: Just the UVF ones. And the UFF ones as well.

Interviewer: Is this your corner?

David and his father.

David: Here's the corner of the house. I just play up there. Playing foot-
ball, so I do.

We walked home with David and spoke with him more about his father. His
mother Karen also took part in the interview.

Interviewer: Can you tell me what happened to your father?

David: He's going out one morning and he was going to do a murder.
Over in Ligonel. And he was going to do a murder. Kill a Catholic,
so he was. But he didn't want to kill him, so he didn't. And he had
police all around him right there, so he did.

Interviewer: So he didn't actually kill anyone that day?

David: He didn't murder a Catholic.

Interviewer: But he got arrested?

David: Yes.

Mother: When he went to the court, he got sixteen years for conspiracy to
murder, attempted murder, possession of firearms, hijacking of a taxi.

Interviewer: David, what do you think about your father's situation?

David: I think the paramilitaries aren't really good, like. Sure, you're

Siblings Danny and Michelle witnessed their father's murder by Protestant paramilitaries.

going out to kill somebody's daddy and he has children, so he does. And you're going to leave them with no daddy and their daddy's going to be dead, so you are. It's just like someone coming into this house shooting my daddy dead. We're left with no daddy. How would somebody else feel doing that?

Mother: He's doing time but I'm doing time with him. And the children, they're doing time with me. Because when I'm feeling down and I'm angry, then I take it out on the kids. And then I would say to myself, they didn't do no harm on me. What am I doing taking it out on my own children?

Interviewer: Are you mad at your father?

David: I guess, I'm sort of. He still didn't want to do it. So he didn't.

For close to five years, David has been visiting his father in the Maze for a few hours each month. He rides with his mother and other Protestant paramilitary prisoner families in a special bus provided by the UVF. Although he looks forward to these trips, the end of the visit always leaves him rather sad to be separated again from his father. David and his mother are hopeful these visits will soon be over. Under the terms of the Good Friday Peace Accord, all paramilitary prisoners from both sides will be released in the year 2000 if their organizations continue to observe a ceasefire.

In recent years, Protestant paramilitary groups have superseded the IRA as the prime killers in the thirty-year "Troubles." Since 1991, the UVF and the UFF have killed more people in Northern Ireland than the IRA. But over the thirty year period, the IRA has killed more in total and has tended to target and murder members of the British security forces. The largest number of sectarian murders have been perpetrated by Protestant paramilitaries.

Two Catholic children whose family fell victim to these Protestant terrorist groups are Danny and Michelle, brother and sister, who live in a Catholic neighborhood that closely borders a Protestant one.

Michelle: There be a lot of fighting with the Protestants and the Catholics who always fight with each other just up the street. And the children would throw stones at each other. They would riot with each other.

Danny: They would throw bricks and stones, you know, at people. And shout abuse.

Interviewer: Why would they do this?

Michelle: Because we don't get on with each other.

Danny: Because we're Catholics and they're Protestants and they just don't like it—us being Catholics.

Interviewer: And that's all it takes?

Danny: That's all it takes.

Interviewer: You live near a Peace Wall and what do you think about that wall? Do you think it's necessary?

Danny and Michelle: Yes.

Interviewer: And you're glad it's there?

Danny and Michelle: Yes. [*They nod their heads.*]

Interviewer: Could you tell me the story about what happened to your father?

Michelle: Well, we lived up the Springfield Road and that was beside a crossroad. There were Protestants who lived across the road from us. And we were going on holiday to Spain in the early hours of that morning. And my mommy and my daddy were getting last minute shopping in before we went.

My mommy and daddy came back from the shopping center and me and Danny were up in the bedroom. And our bedroom was at the front of the house so we could see my daddy and mommy pulling up in the car. Mommy and Daddy got out of the car. My daddy went to the back of the car to take out the shopping bags.

And just then another car pulled up behind our daddy. Five men got out of the car with masks on and guns and shot him. Shot at him. And he fell back and Mommy was standing at the front door. She started screaming and they said, "Be quiet or we'll shoot you too." And then they got into the car and drove away.

Interviewer: This must have been very upsetting to you. Did you have nightmares and bad dreams for a long time?

Danny: Yes. The shock of seeing it left me with a stammer, so it did. And even now I get nightmares over it, you know. Of it ever happening again.

Interviewer: And who did it?

Michelle: The UVF.

Danny: The UVF kill and bomb Catholics.

Interviewer: Did anyone ever get arrested?

Michelle: I think two men got arrested. Two of the men.

Interviewer: And were they sent to prison?

Danny and Michelle: No. No.

Interviewer: What do you think of the men who did it?

Michelle: I always used to say to my mommy, "I hate the men who killed my daddy." But my mommy taught me to forgive them. She taught us to forgive them and not to hold a grudge against them for what they did. She says, "If you keep on hating them, it will only tear yourself apart. You'll only hurt yourself more."

Rodney, left, at the Lagan School.

Interviewer: What would you tell children who've never experienced such a thing?

Michelle: I would say that it's hard but that you have to be strong. You have to be a strong person.

Danny: To cope with it all.

Michelle: And you just have to get on with your life.

Danny: Make the best of it.

The Lagan School was the first integrated school in Northern Ireland. This secondary school, located in Castlereagh just outside of Belfast, was started in 1981 by a parents' organization. Nine hundred Catholic and Protestant children attend the school in equal numbers. We observed that integrated school children can talk freely about politics. Many integrated students do not have the entrenched political views of other children in Northern Ireland. This discussion took place in a class of fifteen-year-old boys and girls at the school. We did, however, observe that this age group was less naïve in their hopes for the peace process.

Rodney: I have changed my views a bit and have come down from being totally bigoted to being only really slightly bigoted. So I have changed my views and think this school has helped me to re-

Students from the Lagan School.

alize that Catholic people are just as normal as me. I have changed a bit anyway.

Carrie: You know, I don't think anybody here has really political views. It's more what they believe is right and what's wrong...a moral point of view. But you know we do listen to what other people have to say. And we just try to decide for ourselves what we think is right and what we think is wrong.

Girl Student 1: You've got to respect Rodney's views. Everybody has a view and he has a right to them. If we don't agree with him, it's just our view and his view. We don't fight over anything.

Interviewer: Do you think that is what's happened by coming to this school? Is this something you've learned because you've come to this school? How to respect one another?

Class: Yeah. Yeah.

Interviewer: Well, right now we have political talks going on that may lead to a Peace Accord in Northern Ireland. Do you see that as a possibility for peace?

Carrie: I really can't see it end, you know, in another fifty, seventy-five years...whatever, you know. Not in my lifetime. Like I've always hoped for peace to come and will continue hoping. But I can never see it come to a complete end and there never being another shooting or never being another bomb. You know there's always going to be the fear there that something's going to go wrong again.

Interviewer: You have that fear now?

Carrie: Yeah. I think the people always have the fear that something's going to happen, especially something either to them or to their family. Because you know it isn't as if they're going after just the other paramilitaries. They're going after the public. Anybody could be shot down or bombed even by accident, at any time.

Interviewer: How many of you would like to leave Northern Ireland when you finish school? [*Most of the children in the class raised their hands to indicate that they would someday leave Northern Ireland.*]

Girl Student 2: I want to go down to Dublin. Because I'd like to go down there. Because, I mean, obviously I don't want to stay here all my life. It's like staying in a rut. You know what I mean? When I'm older and when I get married, if I do get married and settle down with kids, I don't want them to grow up here. It's just that a lot of kids nowadays have a lot of hatred for each other. And there's so much conflict. And I just don't want my kids to be like that. So I just

want them to get out of this place. You know, it's just too much violence, basically.

Carrie: Well, I always thought whenever the Troubles were bad, I always
thought I'd like to move to England to get away from it. But I don't
want to move any more. I want to stay here. You know, all my family's here, all my friends are here. You just have to keep on living
your life as normal as possible.

Three months after the Peace Accord was signed in April 1998, the
British government sent troops once again to block the Orange Order's
Drumcree Parade from marching past Catholic homes on the Garvaghy
Road in Portadown. This time, in response to the parade ban, Protestant
paramilitaries set fire to ten Catholic churches. The RUC believed the
arson to be the work of a dissident Protestant paramilitary group calling itself the Loyalist Volunteer Force (LVF). The LVF is opposed to the peace
process in Northern Ireland.

Several days later, Protestant paramilitaries also firebombed the home of
Richard, Mark, and Jason Quinn. The three Catholic brothers, aged eight,
nine, and eleven, burned to death as they slept in their beds. The family had
been targeted because the boys' Catholic mother was living with a Protestant
man and the boys were attending a Protestant school. The terrible incident
shocked both Catholic and Protestants throughout Northern Ireland.

In the sermon read at the boys' funeral, Father Peter Forde told the con-
gregation, "Richard, Mark, and Jason are at home. We meet in sorrow at the
deaths of these children, but our shared sorrow is a beacon of hope for our
community. In this our very troubled country, may it light our way ahead."

The fragile peace accord suffered yet another attack one month later. A
powerful car bomb ripped through the busy shopping center of Omagh, a re-
ligiously mixed community fifty miles west of Belfast. A splinter group calling itself "the Real IRA" took credit for the blast. The Real IRA, a terrorist
group opposed to the Peace Accord, was made up of dissident members of
the IRA who left the group in anger after the Irish Republican Army observed a ceasefire in 1997. Twenty-nine people were killed and 220 injured in
the bombing. It was the deadliest attack ever in the history of the "Troubles." The horrific terrorist attack paralyzed the peace process and led to
fears that Northern Ireland would once again be plunged into another dark
era of sectarian violence.

In December of 1999, the government of Northern Ireland was returned to

Belfast, ending twenty-seven years of direct rule from London. After nineteen months of agonizing struggle, Protestant and Catholic politicians finally agreed to a power-sharing government. The implementation of the Peace Accord once again holds the promise of an end to violence in Northern Ireland. For the children of the "Troubles," it is long overdue. May they live the rest of their lives growing up in a country finally at peace.

Richard, Mark, and Jason Quinn, ages 8, 9, and 11.
ABOVE: *The funeral for the three boys.*

CHILDREN IN WAR CODA

How many times must innocents die?

War violates every right of a child.

–The right to life

–The right to health and education

–The right to be with family and community

–The right to live in peace.

Who will listen to the voices of the children?

We are not just witnesses to their fate but participants.

It is the moral responsibility of a civilized world to protect the rights of children.

At the end of the twentieth century, targeting and killing
children in war is still a crime against humanity.

afterword

Nothing really prepares you for going to a war zone. You busy yourself with trying to organize the complex travel arrangements and formidable production filming logistics. You do research and consult with experts in an effort to understand the history of the conflicts in each country. You talk to the workers at relief agencies who have recently returned from war zones. You confer with child psychologists in an effort to understand the effects of armed conflict and terrorism on children. You study Fielding's travel guide *The World's Most Dangerous Places,* and note with caution that each of the four countries you are about to visit has a lengthy chapter devoted to it. You try to prepare as best you can. But in the end the journey has little to do with camera equipment, visas, or press badges. The jolting reality of actually traveling to war-torn countries such as Bosnia and Rwanda was another experience, one that compared with nothing in our prior filming encounters.

On our first trip to Rwanda, we flew in an old Russian cargo plane delivering United Nations relief supplies from Nairobi, Kenya. At that time, there were few commercial flights into Rwanda. The flight lasted a little over two hours; there were no seats or windows on the plane, which had definitely seen better days. We wrapped ourselves in plastic webbing which hung from the plane's ceiling, and hoped for the best. Arriving in Kigali, we noticed that all the glass in the airport's windows had been shot out by artillery fire. Soldiers with automatic rifles, speaking only French, slowly examined our luggage and asked why we were visiting the country. No one was meeting us at the airport to provide any assistance.

Because we were working as independent filmmakers and not as part of a large network or cable news organization, we were pretty much on our own and had to focus on our survival instincts. We didn't carry satellite telephones because there was no one to call if we got into trouble. Driving through the ravaged streets of Kigali in a beat-up African taxi to the Hotel des Mille Collines, we made mental notes of all the things we had to do. Arriving in each country, we had to figure out where to stay, negotiate the local currency, rent cars, hire translators, drivers, and film crew assistants, obtain government press credentials, and quickly assess which parts of town to avoid and at what times. There was no functioning banking system in either Bosnia or Rwanda during our filming. This necessitated carrying large amounts of cash on our bodies. Although nothing ever happened to us because of this, it was just one more anxiety-producing aspect of the production.

Although it was reassuring to carry "body armor" with us—both flak jackets and bullet-resistant Kevlar vests—we rarely, if ever, wore them. They were heavy and cumbersome, making it difficult to operate the 16mm camera and sound recorder. In hindsight, Rwanda was probably the most dangerous of the four countries we traveled to, especially at night, when we were driving back from the Zaire (now Congo) border and were often stopped at makeshift roadblocks by young men in military dress who carried automatic rifles. Were they government soldiers there to ensure our safety? Or were they members of the Hutu *Interahamwe?* You can pretend to be brave under such circumstances, but it is a very frightening moment. We had to mentally train ourselves to work through such experiences, to keep our fears and anxiety under control, to not think too much about how truly far away we were from a safe haven.

Our first days in Mostar, Bosnia-Herzegovina, were similarly disillusioning. We were preparing ourselves to deal with traumatized children but quickly realized that the entire city's population was traumatized. Most of Mostar had been shelled into ruins. Hospitals, mosques, churches, and schools had been the primary targets of the artillery attacks. Symbolically, there was a huge explosion hole on the side of the city's main hospital, right below the building's International Red Cross insignia. Freshly dug graves were everywhere.

There were no hotels for us to stay in; each day we had to drive back and forth to Mostar from a neighboring city over a treacherous mountain road in an armored vehicle. The armored vehicle was necessary because the Serbian army had numerous artillery bunkers dug into the hillside high above the city. At any time they could fire a volley at vehicles trying to enter Mostar. We vividly remember going to get our press credentials in a gloomy and cold government building, standing on line with some of the most anguished looking men and women we had ever seen. They were there seeking transit papers that would allow them to travel to the other side of the city so they could locate their missing family members. The line moved very slowly but everyone waited patiently, apparently resigned to their terrible fates. It seemed to us that we had been miraculously transported back in time to some World War II battleground. It was hard to comprehend that this horrific urban landscape exists today.

The real journey, however, began when we met the children. It was necessary to find translators who would assist us in interviewing the boys and girls we intended to film. Making a film in five different languages—Serbo-Croatian, Hebrew, Arabic, Kinyarwandan, and English—only one of which we spoke, was perhaps the greatest challenge in filming the documentary. It is also a difficult process to speak with children through interpreters while at the same time encouraging them to talk openly about their war-related experiences. We feared we might be delving into painful areas for the children. But the child psychologists we consulted during our research had, without exception, encouraged us to get the children to talk openly about the terrible events they had lived through. By freely expressing themselves in this way, the children could begin to take control of the traumatic incidents they witnessed. As the stories started to unfold, tales of murder and other atrocities were described. At first it was difficult not to shed a tear or simply stop filming because of the horror of the events being recounted. We soon learned that we had to be as brave as the children.

Working with children is a very rewarding experience because they are extremely honest in their feelings. They will look you straight in the eye and give you the most direct and intimate answers to complicated questions. They have experienced as much violence as any soldier in combat. In many cases the simple act of running away and hiding had saved their lives. The instinct to survive is in all of us and it is amazing to see children as young as five having to act on this impulse.

All of the children we interviewed, no matter what age, were completely aware of the political forces affecting their lives. They did not speak of hate or revenge but longed for the time when peace would return to their country. They were not naïve victims whose allegiance and support had been gained through bullying, harassment, or violence. They all spoke of the need for justice and the punishment of their aggressors.

There were, of course, some children who simply couldn't speak or who were unable to retell their personal stories. Some children would start to stutter or sob uncontrollably and we would have to console them. In times of war, the relief agencies and children's parents are most concerned with dire necessities like food, shelter, and medical assistance. There are very few materials devoted to helping with the children's psychological wounds. Few schools in war zones have the materials available to offer art therapy sessions or other counseling for children in war. Yet the boys and girls must be reached as soon as possible before their post–traumatic stress disorder becomes deeply ingrained in their personalities. It was apparent in many situations that we had been the first to ask the children to talk about the loss of their parents or homeland. The interview sessions would often produce an immediate group response of support for one another. Other children and adults would gather around to listen to the stories the children were telling and find some small reassurance that they shared a common personal history.

The children of Bosnia and Rwanda experienced some of the worst violence and atrocities of the twentieth century. The children of Bosnia had lost their homes, their fathers, and had barely escaped the brutal ethnic cleansing policy of both the Serbs and the Croats. The deliberate targeting of children by snipers or armed militias was particularly difficult for us to comprehend. Psychoanalysts explain this military tactic as a means of dehumanizing the enemy and seeing children merely as "cockroaches" or "little rats." After hearing numerous eyewitness accounts of these atrocities, the comment made by twelve-year-old Muslim refugee, Selma, seemed the only meaningful explanation: "Some people wish us evil."

We will forever have a place in our hearts for the children of Rwanda. The boys and girls of this small, impoverished African country fell victim to another historical genocide, the most evil of all crimes. Hundreds of thousands of them were left orphaned and homeless, and a vast majority witnessed the murder of parents and siblings by brutal machete blows. Their accounts of death and torture were almost unbearable to hear. The children showed extraordinary courage and ingenuity while escaping the Hutu *Interhamwe* killers. Living in

the safety of America, we can't begin to comprehend their experiences. When young Uwamuhoza told us, "We were hiding. My dad, my mom, and myself. And they came and killed us. They cut me with a machete and killed me," she was in her way expressing a profound truth.

At an orphanage, we stood before a large group of children performing a song they wrote entitled "You Can't Imagine How We Managed to Survive," and we were overwhelmed with sadness and admiration. These boys and girls were the true survivors of war and were the future generation of their country. How would they ever overcome such trauma? Would they forgive and live together with their Hutu neighbors again? Who would educate them for the task of governing their country? This monumental undertaking was left to these child survivors. We like to believe that they will again show great strength of character and rebuild their lives.

The experience of talking to children who have never known peace in their lifetime is shocking and in many ways incomprehensible. In Israel, three generations of children have grown up in a country where there is the constant threat of terrorism and a legacy of state-sponsored abuse toward the Palestinians. The vast majority of Arab and Israeli children never come into direct contact with on another and they know little about each other's daily life or culture. Yet all of the children in Israel are politicized and have strong feelings about the future of their country. The stress that this can place on young children is all too apparent; in our observation as journalists, too many Arab and Israeli children seem worldly-wise at a young age. Palestinian boys and girls would invariably tell us that they could never forgive the Israelis for what they had done to their people. Israeli children expressed no desire to get to know their Palestinian neighbors. Such finite and negative declarations do not offer a great deal of hope for their future. If children today on both sides of the Arab-Israeli divide cannot envision a future of living together peacefully, how many more generations will be caught in this politicized cycle of violence?

As we were preparing to leave the American Colony Hotel in Jerusalem on the first morning of our filming, a Hamas suicide bomber blew up a crowded bus in Jerusalem carrying Israeli soldiers and civilians to work. This incident, which occurred blocks from our hotel, set the stage for the Israeli portion of our documentary. Arriving on the scene, we observed that the army quickly reacted to the incident, providing emergency medical services to the few surviving victims. That day the Israeli broadcast media saturated the country with messages of outrage directed at the terrorists and sympathy for the victims of the attack. It seemed that all of the people of Israel were grieving together. Nonetheless, over the next few days, the country returned to its normal routine as if to demonstrate that it would not be paralyzed or intimidated by the bombing. On the second week of our visit, another Palestinian terrorist bomb exploded on another crowded bus. The public outcry this time was louder and angrier but the same actions were taken by the army and the same public grieving took place. It became apparent that this was the accepted form of behavior during such tragedies.

By this time, the Israeli army had imposed what they term "closure" on most of the roads leading to Gaza and other West Bank cities. Our scheduled visit to Gaza's Jabalia refugee camp was canceled due to the recent bombing incidents. After a frenzied week of phone calls to make new arrangements and seek permissions, we were once again on our way to Gaza. As we sat in line at the border to have our Israeli government press credentials checked, a third terrorist bomb exploded in Tel Aviv in a bustling shopping mall. Sitting in our car and knowing we were never going to Gaza that day, we watched as Israeli army bulldozers erected a huge wall in the Mediterranean to close off access to the sea. We had never seen a country closed with such swift efficiency and determination. Yet, at the same time, the Israeli army seemed powerless to stop the terrorist attacks.

We eventually did gain access to Gaza and Hebron, and filmed the reactions of Palestinian children. Many of them accepted terrorist bombings as a normal and justifiable reaction to past Israeli actions, and few of the Arab boys and girls believed that the peace process would ever improve their lives. Back in Israel, we followed the story of a nine-year-old Russian immigrant boy named

Vladik who had lost both his parents in the first of the three bus bombings that occurred during our filming. He was a difficult interview, not saying too much. But when we asked him the last thing he remembered saying to his parents that morning, he smiled broadly and said *"Lehitra"* which means "See ya!"

After finishing the filming of two different funerals for very young children, we found it increasingly difficult to keep our composure. We had heard too many stories of murder and deliberate targeting of children, and we had been visiting far too many gravesites. The film was beginning to take its toll on us.

Our trip to Northern Ireland, for our final filming, was based on the hopeful prospects of the ongoing Peace Accord negotiations. It would be important to show how the struggle for peace was affecting the children of Northern Ireland and their hope for their future. As in Israel, generations of boys and girls had grown up in Northern Ireland knowing nothing but the thirty-year-long Troubles.

We made a documentary for ABC News in 1980 about the role of the British Army and the IRA. That year was the worst of times in Northern Ireland; there was a continual IRA terrorist bombing campaign while British soldiers heavily patrolled the streets and intimidated the Catholic population. Sixteen years later, we returned to a country that appeared to have experienced great prosperity. The IRA had maintained a ceasefire for seventeen months and the mood was hopeful that peace at last would come to this troubled land. The British government had upgraded public housing, unemployment had decreased, and there was a small initiative to integrate the divided cultures of Protestants and Catholics. There were no more security gates surrounding the shops in the city's center and a host of international chain stores like Disney and Conran's had moved in. We once again checked into the Europa in Belfast which has the dubious distinction of being the world's most bombed hotel. The Europa was bombed thirty times in the 1970s, mostly by the IRA. A huge blast in 1993 almost destroyed it, but here it was again, all fixed up. Even President Clinton had stayed here.

Although we had high hopes for a somewhat positive final sequence in our documentary, events quickly altered that plan. On the first day of our filming, in an eerie parallel to our experience in Israel, the IRA broke their seventeen-month ceasefire and set off a large truck bomb in a shopping center in Manchester, England. The blast was apparently motivated by the poor treatment Sinn Fein, the political wing of the IRA, felt they were receiving at Stormont Castle where the Peace Accord talks were being held. Overnight, Northern Ireland was plunged back into conflict.

As we drove around Belfast, going to both Catholic and Protestant neighborhoods, we began to have the feeling that maybe things hadn't really changed that much in the last twenty years. Neighborhoods that had previously been separated by makeshift barbed wire barricades were now permanently divided by eighteen-foot-high brick walls. The same picturesque, albeit sinister, political graffiti was still prominently displayed on the walls of buildings to clearly mark the territory's religious allegiance. Although we saw no British soldiers on patrol, the RUC officers stopping traffic at surprise roadblocks around the city carried what looked like machine guns.

We interviewed seventeen-year-old Karen, daughter of a convicted IRA bomber who, stating her strong belief in the just cause of the Irish Republican Army, used the same anti-British political rhetoric we could have recorded in 1980. We wondered how this country was ever going to shed its dark legacy and finally look to the future. David, the eleven-year-old son of an Ulster Defense Force (UDF) prisoner jailed for the attempted murder of a Catholic, said he wanted no part of the paramilitaries when he grows up. Yet printed on every other wall in his neighborhood on the Shankill Road were pictures of hooded men carrying automatic weapons and pledging to uphold the Red Hand of Ulster. Would David survive these streets and resist the temptation to be drawn into the violent world of the paramilitary groups? We hoped so but it appeared that at least some of Northern Ireland's children of the Troubles were still deeply embedded in the past.

We tried reaching out to a small group of parents and their children who had started the integrated school movement in Belfast. To our relief, when talking with these students, we could see a difference in their outlook for the future. The integrated school children were learning how to live together and how to accept each other's different points of view. But as the classroom discussion continued, we learned of their desire to leave their homes in Northern Ireland because they had no confidence that things would ever really change. Many of them spoke of moving to Dublin or other European cities. "There's so much conflict," one fifteen-year-old student said. "And I just don't want my kids to be like that. So I just would want them to get out of this place. It's just too much violence, basically."

This was a far cry from the hope expressed in the touching essays written by the eleven-year-olds at the integrated primary school. Who was right in predicting the future? We knew how fragile the struggle for peace can be but we were hopeful for a positive ending to our film. We could never have foreseen the violent sectarian acts of the following summer when Protestant paramilitaries firebombed three Catholic brothers, aged eight, nine, and eleven, as they slept in their beds. The horrific murders of these innocent boys, so senseless and so brutal, was heartbreaking. The terrifying Real IRA bombing in the busy city center of Omagh that followed a month later showed that Northern Ireland had once more been "sucked into that desolate moral vacuum" that Graca Machel so eloquently described.

However, with the implementation of the Peace Accord at the end of 1999, there is once again hope for the end of violence and a lasting peace for the Children of the Troubles.

As we witness the end of our violent century, in which our culture seems to be increasingly superficial and self-involved, the treatment of the world's children is perhaps one of the last remaining moral tests of our global society. If we have no regard for children's safety, their lives or their future, what does that say about us? We made "Children in War" to force viewers to confront this sad reality, to not turn away in indifference. As broadcast journalists we can only try to bring these issues of injustice to a wider audience. It is everyone's moral responsibility to ensure a child's right to peace. Our society must strive for a global conscience, a compassionate effort to attain a modern world culture of universal human rights for children. It is in the commitment to protect children that hope for the future lies.

acknowledgments

We would like to extend our deepest gratitude to the children of Bosnia, Israel, Rwanda, and Northern Ireland for sharing their stories with us. They displayed enormous patience with the oftentimes tedious process of speaking through interpreters and were willing to talk about their war experiences. They all gave honest and insightful answers to our probing and sometimes intimate questions. They acted with enormous strength and dignity under the worst conditions. Without them this book would not have been possible. We also must thank their teachers, mothers, and fathers who assisted us with their trust and support.

We are indebted to Sheila Nevins, our executive producer at Home Box Office, for believing in our feature documentary "Children In War" and sustaining us during the more than four years it took to produce. Sheila also offered guidance, wisdom, and advice, challenging us to make the best possible film we could. Also at HBO we are grateful to John Hoffman, our supervising producer, for his enthusiasm, attention to detail, and genuine concern for us. Home Box Office is to be commended for having the seriousness of purpose to put programs like "Children In War" on the air.

Our thanks also to Everett Ressler, our advisor on the project. Everett provided us with his invaluable insight into the plight of children growing up in war zones. His lasting commitment to helping the world's children caught in armed conflict is truly admirable.

We are also grateful to the many international relief workers who took the time to help us, especially in Bosnia and Rwanda. Special thanks to Danielle Maillefer and Rune Stuvland at the UNICEF area office for former Yugoslavia, Geoff Wiffin at the UNICEF field office Mostar, and to William Hetzer, UNICEF Information Office U.S.A.

In Rwanda we wish to thank Nasser Ega Musa, UNICEF Kigali Information Office; Anne Sophie Bonefeld, International Red Cross Kigali; Leanne McCowan and the Rev. Martin Nzaramba, Compassion International;

acknowledgments

Aimable Sendarasi, Village D'Enfants S.O.S. Kigali; Crispin Sinanyigaya, Gitagata Boy's Facility; and Patrick Kashenshebusca, CUAMM Nyamata.

Our thanks also to Dr. Eyad El-Serraj, Gaza Community Mental Health Program; Fryal Abu Haiklal headmistress of the Quortaba Elementary School Hebron; and to Noam Arnon of the Jewish Community of Hebron. In Northern Ireland, our thanks go to Mildred Kennedy, headmistress Forge Integrated Primary School Belfast; B.K. Lambkin, head the Lagan Integrated School Castlereigh; and to the community offices of Sinn Fein and the Ulster Volunteer Force.

The documentary and book could not have been made without the considerable assistance of our group of translators including Boris Beck, Zeljka Markic, Ivana Nizich, Ruthy Zuta, Shachar Baron, Nael Shuyoukhi, Asya Abdul Hadi, Bana Sayeh, Rula Amin, Gabriel Asfar, Tarsis Karugarama, and Aimable Twagilimana.

Finally we wish to thank our son for his endless patience and goodwill in putting up with our long absences from home during the months of research and filming travel. His youthful forbearance during the intense times of the editing of the documentary and the writing of this book are to be commended.

about the authors

Academy Award®-winning filmmakers Alan and Susan Raymond have produced and directed feature-length documentaries for Public Television, ABC News, Home Box Office (HBO), the Disney Channel, and the BBC in England. Their most recently completed documentary is "Children in War," a feature-length study of the tragic consequences of war and terrorism for the children of Bosnia, Israel, Rwanda, and Northern Ireland. It premiered on HBO in January 2000.

The Raymonds' previous film, *I Am a Promise: The Children of Stanton Elementary School,* chronicled a year in the life of a troubled inner-city elementary school in North Philadelphia. This film has been honored with an Oscar® for Best Feature Documentary of 1994, a Prime Time Emmy® Award for Outstanding Information Special, a George Foster Peabody Award, an Alfred I. DuPont Award from the Columbia School of Journalism and a First Prize Robert F. Kennedy Journalism Award for Television Reporting.

The Raymonds specialize in long-form social-issue documentaries. They have produced films on education and schooling, mental illness, policing in America, juvenile justice, prison reform, the British Army and the IRA in Northern Ireland, as well as historical documentaries on urban blues music in Chicago and the early days of rock and roll with Elvis Presley. The Raymonds were also the filmmakers of the seminal twelve-hour cinema verité PBS documentary series, *An American Family.*

Many of the Raymonds' films are part of the permanent collections of museums and public libraries such as the Museum of Modern Art and the Museum of Broadcasting in New York City, as well as the Bibliotheque National de France in Paris. In 1995, the American Cinematheque in Los Angeles held a retrospective screening of the Raymonds' films. They have been the recipients of an artists grant from the Rockefeller Foundation, received nine Emmy® Awards, and twice have been awarded the George Foster Peabody Award and the Columbia School of Journalism's DuPont Award. They live in the Hudson River Valley, New York.